❧Ackn
To Ou

We wish to thank our special patrons, who helped make the first printing of this possible. Your participation not only supports our efforts as independent author-publishers but also pays homage to a time honored tradition in publishing.

Susan McDonald	Gary McDonald	Melodi Watson
Roz Owen	Susan Clark	Ellen Stone-Belic
Jo Chavez	Karen Gahr	Marjie Serge
Deborah Ingman	Jeff Ingman	Charlie Serge

The **McDonald's** and I spent many hours together making sure we didn't give the IRS too much . . . or too little. Those hours turned a business relationship into a friendship.

Roz Owen and I completed our Graduate work together a few years back, burning the midnight oil and finding a common ground for fellowship that continues to this day.

Susan Clark is one of my oldest clients (not in age, simply in the length of time we've been working together); she's an accomplished horticulturist and a wise friend.

When my spirits are low, I visit my friend and 'coach' **Jo Chavez**, a Medical Intuitive with an impressive ability to heal.

Fellow Network Marketer **Karen Gahr** is by far one of the most enthusiastic people on Planet Earth! When she enters a room, it lights up.

After my graduate work, I did a short stint as a professor where I had the privilege of meeting **Melodi Watson** (one of my students). I took pleasure in her occasional yet enlightening comments and observations.

Ellen Stone-Belic and I met in the summer of 1997 at a writer's workshop. Sitting in a yurt in the middle of a New Mexico desert, a thousand acres from the nearest telephone, we were fellow authors learning to *Write From Our Hearts* and tell our personal story.

The **Ingman's**, also originally tax clients, have become good friends and have always been great real estate scouts.

Marjie Serge is first in our SuccessLine of MLMers as well as, without doubt one of the sweetest and gentlest creatures on the Planet.

Marjie's lovely nine-year-old daughter **Charlie Serge** is what I call *courageous!* This past summer, while jumping on a trampoline in her back yard, she broke her leg in two places (with skin graphs and all!) yet she came through it with great courage and a big Tweetie Bird™.

Thank you for your support and confidence.

Confessions

of a Multi-Level Marketer;
Networking From Your Heart ✐

Written by

Patrick Snetsinger

PALINOIA PRESS ✽ BELLEVUE, WASHINGTON ✽ 1997

ISBN 1-57502-668-6

Printed in the USA by
Morris Publishing
3212 East Hwy. 30
Kearney, NE 68847
1-800-650-7888
First Edition: November 1997

Celebration!

I celebrate the publication of this book with Kris Kegg who is, among her many talents, a gifted editorial consultant, close collaborator, graphic designer and my best friend. I am grateful for her humor, wisdom, constant love, and partnership;

ILY$^\infty$

In memory of my dear Aunt June,
an author in her own right.
July 3, 1924 - October 16, 1997

PROLOGUE

Seems this is a good place for me to tell you why I wrote this book. It started out as 'therapy', a sort of peace of mind for me. New to MLM (Network Marketing), frustrated and yet somehow hopeful, I started journaling my thoughts, feelings, new ideas that I would read about, special conversations I would have with my mentors, as well as my daydreams of success in networking. Soon a book began to emerge from all the words and, after reading it I thought it might just bring a little peace of mind and hopefulness to others. So, there you have it. Nothing more . . . nothing less.

As I copyedit and prepare to mail this manuscript to the publisher, an article written by Dee W. Hock about his view of the future comes to mind. The beginning of his paper sums up my feelings about how important MLM is to the future of our global society. Here are his words for your late night reading pleasure:

> . . . *a new organizational form that carries within it the seeds of a new organizational culture that might well spell the difference between a smooth, orderly transition to a healthful and sustainable global society, and the chaos and anarchy that some see in our near-term future.*[*]

---

[*] Dee Hock wrote this article to encourage traditional corporate America to change before there is anarchy and total collapse.

I like to use quotes to give depth to a particular point or concept. I will, from time-to-time, place such a quote on a separate page in order to give you the opportunity to slow down and absorb whatever it is I'm musing about. I find that exceptionally poignant quotes, when placed on the same page as the main body of the text, frequently do not get pondered properly.

So, I put some of my favorite citations on their own page; please . . . slow down and soak 'em up!

We read books to find out who we are. What other people, real or imaginary, do and think and feel is an essential guide to our understanding of what we ourselves are and may become.
✍ Ursula K. LeGuin

CONTENTS

IN THE BEGINNING...

The story I tell here was inspired by actual events (just like on television). It details my 18-month odyssey as a 49-year-old-first-time networker. As I travel "this road less traveled," I stumble upon insights that bring me face-to-face with *me* (a real shock) and ultimately with success. I approach networking with 23 years of entrepreneurial 'command and control' practice. To my surprise, my MLM experiences range from humorous to tragic to enlightening. My tale is filled with hope and penetrating questions, that may lift you to a universe overflowing with new possibilities and paradigms to ponder.

One day while walking in the forest in solitude, I began wondering if I should continue with this business. I've been told over and over and over that "the only way to fail is to quit." Still, that is exactly what was on my mind. I was tired and my soul worn thin from all the rejection, sneers, pain and humiliation. I felt lost and unsure of which path to travel. In this moment of aloneness and despair, I quietly asked for guidance. Suddenly, in a flash, a new path appeared. This book chronicles my MLM adventure along this new trail.

> *In the middle of the road of my life I awoke in a*
> *dark wood where the true way was wholly lost.*
> ✍ Dante, *Commedia*

Do I believe in network marketing? A roaring YES! I believe this industry is one of many possible solutions to the economic, financial, and social confusion the planet is currently undergoing. Networking is a conceivable link between chaos and potential order -- a model to positively impact the whole planet. It doesn't take a rocket scientist to realize we are in the midst of a global epidemic of institutional failure. Network Marketing just might be our safety net.

From *Conversations with God; book 2,* I offer the following quote as a way to take a first step out into the new paradigm of multi-level marketing.

> *This paradigm shift will take great wisdom, great courage, and massive determination. For fear will strike at the heart of these concepts, and call them false. Fear will eat at the core of these magnificent truths, and render them hollow . . . Yet you will not have, cannot produce, the society of which you have always dreamed unless and until you see with wisdom and clarity the ultimate truth: that what you do to others, you do to yourself; what you fail to do for others, you fail to do for yourself; that the pain of others is your pain, and the joy of others your joy, and that when you disclaim any part of it, you disclaim a part of yourself.*

STOP! Do not read another paragraph until you re-read that quote, putting in your mind's eye your MLM organization.

2

Give people a fact or idea and you enlighten their minds; tell them a story and you touch their souls.

✍ old Hasidic Proverb*

*My pledge? To tell you an enjoyable story, peppered with facts and ideas.

January 15th - What a day! Casey, whom I haven't talked with in several months, shuffled up beside me today and murmured quietly "Snets, I know this looks strange (holding up in front of my face a rather unusual product), but it might make you feel better - will you give it a try?"

I told her I already felt good, and started wondering what the scam was.

She said "some of my customers tell me that their eyesight is improved, they stop snoring, they get a better night's sleep, and they have more energy." With this you might add 2 or 3 hours to your day because of the extra energy it gives you while you're sleeping! You will wake up earlier with a new zest for the day! Try it, it could work for you, too. Then she lowered her voice just enough to let the others in the office know she was about to tell me a secret and I felt a little embarrassed.

"Oh! there is a business opportunity here if you're interested in retiring early or getting out of debt or whatever."

It was that last comment that sent a shiver down my back. I thought "what's she into this time and what is she going to try to sell me?" Out of courtesy I took the stuff and agreed to try it, though I wasn't sure I would!

As we walked back to our desks she turned and said "I'll check back with you in a few days to see how you're doing."

Oops, guess I have to actually use 'em - Ugh!

January 20 - Another run-in with Casey. First question out of her mouth was, "Snets how do you feel after using those unusual products?"

My response was a bit vague because I still have this feeling I'm being handled. In fact this strange "thing" did help. My feet hurt less at the end of the day and my lower back pain seems to be gone. I actually feel like I have had more energy throughout the day! I told Casey that I was feeling a little better and thanked her for thinking of me. She got so excited I was mortified by her public display!

"Come to a meeting tonight" she said. "You'll learn more about the product and our other products and you'll see just how big this thing really is - it's huge! This really is a ground floor opportunity. I've got a tiger by the tail and I'm riding it all the way to the top. Come tonight and you will hear stories about how remarkable this company is and how the product has saved lives - physically and financially! I'll see you at 7:30, OK?"

I was furious with her blatant assumption that I would be interested in her "biz op"! - I've heard those words before - no way!! She was coming on too strong for me; I could not believe how pushy she was. In an effort to put her off, I told her I'd try to make the meeting and asked for directions. She said, "Look Snets, this is important - to me and to you - will you be there or not"?

About that time I wanted to say NO, capital N, capital O. However I got this weird sense from her enthusiasm and the urgency of it all and finally agreed to go to the meeting. I figure if I go now, she'll be off my back. I hope this is the end of it!

January 20 - Around 7:30 PM - I met Casey at the hotel meeting room and she immediately introduced me to a handful of her 'associates'. I soon learned that each time they make a sale, she gets a piece of their commission! Sounds kinda' like that pyramid stuff from years ago to me - I think it was called "the airplane game!"

She pointed to a man on the other side of the crowded room. "See that guy over there? He makes one-hundred fifty thousand per month! Yes, per month, can you imagine? Oh, what I'd do with that kind of money!

That young man coming up the stairs was a truck mechanic just 5 years ago; today he makes $50,000 a month. And that guy in the lime-colored shirt used to sell house paint - now he's at the top of the pile at $250,000 per month! And see that lady leaning against the wall? A few years ago she was unable to move because of a stroke - now she's a world class downhill skier. WOW! What an opportunity: help people feel better and make mouth-watering profits, obscene sums of money."

The guest speaker, Paul, was a man who joined the ranks of MLM out of kindness to a friend. Actually, he joined to keep his friend from giving him the same old sales pitch, which was wearing thin. Paul explained to us how he casually mentioned the products to his friends and family and how his organization (and paychecks) grew without his direct participation. Sounds too good to be true and yet . . . I wonder, could it be true?

"One day my sponsor called" Paul said "and told me to check my sales volume. I was about to qualify for a new income level (extra bonuses) without even knowing it. That's how easy this business can be; just tell two people a day about your product for a year and you'll be helping perhaps thousands of people feel better while earning 'residual' income."

Residual income means you earn it "whether you roll out of bed in the morning or roll-over". I wonder, could I really just rollover in the morning and earn a living? This paradigm shift they all refer to is not business as usual but instead, working from your home office selling dreams, goods and services.

It took me about 20 minutes to make up my mind . . . I want a piece of the action! I am willing to do, for a few years, what most people won't do in order to live the "good life". On top of that, I'll be helping many people! This feels good -- like a win-win situation. I did it -- I completed the application form, attached my entry fee (thanks to Uncle VISA) and faxed it into the company. I've made the commitment! I have a feeling of incredible hope, excitement, and expectation!

Soon, I will be making more in a month than I've ever dreamed of earning in one year. I am learning that As a MLMer, my role is to help as many people as possible shed their conditioning, and become members of a new way of doing business that is yearning to be born. It's a huge responsibility, and I'm ready for it! I realize now, as I write these words, that I am accomplishing my role through this book.

"SHOW ME THE MONEY!"

That's what I heard at my first meeting and what I kept hearing at subsequent "business briefings" throughout the following year. I realize that's how it started for me . . . the lure of unimaginable sums of money that could be mine if only I would talk with two new people each day about my MLM (Multi-Level Marketing) product.

Before network marketing, and for most of my adult life, I had been self-employed as an accountant. I recently sold my business after 23 years of working it . . . and it working me. I guess I was looking for something else to do. I was not ready to retire, I probably never will be. It was an easy decision to plug network marketing into my life 'cause I had the time, had a great product experience, and believed a new way of delivering goods and services was underway. I wanted to be a part of it.

Jean Houston calls this shift "Jump Time" – a time of historical discontinuity when old paradigms are crumbling and whole new cultures [ways of organizing] are emerging. It is my belief, too, that we are at that point in time when a two-hundred-year-old age is dying and another is struggling to be born.

Ahead, the possibility of regeneration of individuality, liberty, community, and ethics such as the world has never known and a harmony with nature, with one another, and with the divine intelligence such as the world has never dreamed.

✍ Dee Hock

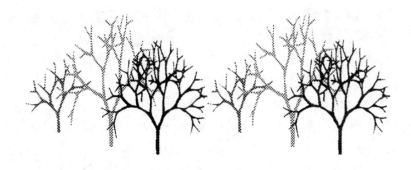

February 15 --I've spent the past three weeks reading all I can get my hands on about this multi-level marketing concept, now referred to as network marketing. Guess this switch to a new name is meant to distance "us" from "them". We are the new guard, taking this form of business into the next millennium. Our past is full of colorful characters who didn't always exercise the common definition of ethics and morality. Seems since about 1934, multi-level marketing has swindled the public and delivered goods & services in an irresponsible manner. The industry has deceived distributors by telling them they will all be earning more money than they can possibly spend -- OH! What am I getting into? Is it the lure of BIG easy money? Or is it truly that I feel this shift happening at a very subtle level and I want to help others make the change? Whatever it is -- it feels right! In the past few weeks I've met people who are sincere, caring, loving, happy, fun to be around. My company and its product *has been around for over 20 years and the physical results are 'real' and amazing. I can't wait to get started!*

February 20 - I'm so excited I can hardly get to sleep at night. My research has yielded a secret "formula" for certain success...

1. *Become a product of the product - by using my company's products, I will be able to honestly tell potential recruits about the benefits.*
2. *Make a list of 100 people - these are the ones I am willing to talk with about my business opportunity and product.*
3. *Get in front of 20 quickly - take along the person who recruited you (your upline) for training.*
4. *Talk with two new people each day about the "biz-op" and the product - the promise: One year from now you'll be earning 'adult wages' as a friend of mine puts it.*

February 22 - WOW!! This is so easy, like falling off a log. I will buy company products, make my list, schedule time with my 'upline' and the prospects on my list! I feel eager to call my friends, neighbors, clients, and family to let them in on this great secret of MLM and of course the product. In light of my enthusiasm, I am certain each of them will see this paradigm shift as easily as I. After all I'm ordinary and I see it, so it's only natural for me to assume they will too.

February 23 - My first effort on the phone yesterday scheduling appointments was a 'bust' a real disaster! After a few calls I realized my list of friends, family, and clients thought I was crazy, or greedy, or that I was having a mid-life crisis (without the sports car)! I remember when Casey first approached me how I felt. I didn't want her to "handle" me or sell me something I didn't want, or coerce me to do something out of my comfort zone. My 'list' is treating me the same way.

I now know what homeostasis is! It's when friends and family exhibit very erratic behavior in order to keep loved ones on the "straight & narrow" - using their definition of course. In fairness, they don't want me to get hurt and yet it seems they don't want me to succeed by doing something 'outside-the-box'!

Insight!

The balancing act for the MLM entrepreneur is to continue loving the customers, friends and family while still being courageous enough to break out of the mold in which they want to keep you.

A NEW WORLD ORDER!

As a Networker you *will* encounter people who disagree with your MLM view (I sure did!). People will *re*-act to you with their model (paradigm) of the world in their mind so your only responsibility is to inform them about your product and the business opportunity. It's up to them to decide what to do with that information. If you pressure or try to persuade them, you will learn what we mean by "if you have to drag 'em in, you will have to drag 'em around." On some occasions, when your prospect is in a reasonable state of mind, you might consider explaining that people's ideas of what's "right" change over and over again from culture to culture, religion to religion, place to place; even family to family. It was once considered "right" to burn people at the stake for what was thought of as witchcraft.

Franchising was once considered illegal, a scam. In 1978, Congress made franchising legal by a mere eleven votes! Today, franchising in North America accounts for over $700 billion dollars in sales with 4,000 franchisers in 600,000 locations. "Right" and "wrong" seem to change with the times, maybe even with the geographic location.

Perhaps 20 years from now you, having started in MLM in 1997, will be in the same financial position that the owners of the local franchises are in today. Twenty years ago these franchise owners took a risk just like you and climbed outside the box. They discovered another way to do business and, along the way, they were shunned, laughed at, threatened with lawsuits, and ridiculed. Today they are the ones smiling and making large deposits in their bank accounts.

February 25 - Because of my telephone rejections I have thought about how I might approach the people on my list with more conscious respect and consideration. It occurs to me that each person on my list is a unique individual and I would be honoring them if I didn't treat each with the same sales approach.

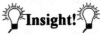

Insight!

Making 'first-contact?'

Why not write a letter to family members and anyone on your 'chicken list' (those who you are afraid to call)? Instead of getting *in their face*, describe the benefits of your product(s) and why you've chosen to represent the company via US mail.

TAILOR MADE

The main point of a "friendly letter" is to keep in touch, as my fifth grade teacher once told me. The main point of this "friendly letter" is to let people know about the product (what it does, why it's unique, etc.), your new company, and why you're involved. It can also ensure them that you won't "hunt them down" to become distributors or retail customers.

Personally, I would exempt family and friends from the "pitch" of MLM. However, it is very important (critical in fact) to tell everyone you know about what you're doing in MLM. Think about who you're going to tell your story to and tailor the presentation suitably. For some, the "in-person" approach will work best, for others a letter will take care of the message. A general sensitivity toward others is a good thing, and MLM gives you many opportunities to hone that skill.

Here's a true story about why it's important to tell *everyone* about your new venture:

> A woman joins an MLM company and begins her climb up the success ladder. After a few years she's making over $10,000 a month. She now has the financial courage to tell her lawyer brother what she's doing. "Darn, I wish you'd told me last year," he said. "I joined MLM CelTel and, at this point, can't justify leaving to start over in your company." In his second year, 'brother dear' grossed $300,000! Had his sister sent him a letter, he might have responded to her product and company, and today her income would be positively affected by his.

21

February 28 - It's 7:30 PM and I'm tired, worn out, and apprehensive. This morning, with new insight, I went back to my list of names intending to treat each person with respect. I was surprised at how difficult it was for me to pick up the phone - how fearful I was about asking for an appointment. I wonder if other MLMers have this experience. Overnight, that ordinary household telephone, gained enormous weight, several hundred pounds in fact. I could hardly lift it! Why is it that I use the phone without thought when I am seeking information or giving news or advice to a friend or colleague? The truth? After a few months in the trenches I think I've discovered that I am scared, afraid of rejection, pure and simple.

Insight!

Right from the start of your MLM career, be conscious of how you work with or against rejection - and know that the people you recruit (your downline) might bump into the same wall.

March 11 thru 13 -- My MLM company provides a week-end training seminar that's designed to improve self esteem and increase belief in self. I attended this seminar with 150 other distributors and, during the three days, there was hardly any mention of our company's name or the products. This training was designed for me, just me, and I entered the training with my usual caution about meeting new people, but I quickly warmed to the others and the shared desire to improve our businesses as well as ourselves. At the end of the seminar, I felt and believed that nothing could stop me from standing at the top. I left the workshop feeling so "pumped" that I fully expect to be earning $10,000 per month by the end of the summer, just six months in the future!

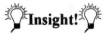
Insight!

External motivation has a shelf-life of about three weeks.

TO FAIL IS TO SUCCEED

I have identified some possible reasons why folks fail at MLM. Would you like me to let you in on my findings? Of course, that's why you're reading this book, right? Okay, here it is! Plain and simple. Most people are externally, rather than internally motivated! In order to succeed in MLM, it's my belief that one must be *internally* enlivened.

An **ex**ternally motivated person is accustomed to being instructed, directed, supervised, and supported on a consistent basis. Sounds like an employee, student, or perhaps a few politicians, eh? MLM cannot provide this, it is not within the nature of the business. Networking is built on the concept of duplicable systems. I recruit you and teach you to recruit, and you teach your recruit to recruit and teach, and so it goes. The hand-holding honeymoon period is short by the very nature of networking. When an externally motivated person is recruited they may find it difficult to duplicate the process, and may, unfortunately, fail.

OK, next question. Where does this internal motivation come from? You may even wonder, how can I get some? Well, it doesn't come cheap. It takes hard work and desire, yet that's all it takes. And the hard work isn't that hard after all. Later, we'll discuss how individuals respond to adversity and how to increase your *desire* for success. Then, with lots of practice you can turn away from the need for external supervision, instruction, and support; you <u>can</u> become more self-reliant. I know that's a big promise, but I also know, when you *feel* desire in your heart, you will become *addicted* to internal motivation.

Given the right circumstances, from no more than dreams, determination [desire], and the liberty to try, quite ordinary people consistently do extraordinary things.*

                   ✍ Dee Hock

*I've seen the truth of this statement many times over in the ranks of my MLM company.

March 20 - Last week-end, at the company sponsored training, I learned how to visualize my future and thereby create it! I was taught how to make a "personal treasure map" comprised of all the things I want and all the attitudes I want. My map was constructed on a piece of card stock 3 feet by 18". I collected several, maybe 30, different magazines and cut out and pasted onto the board anything and everything I wanted. All of it!! The seminar leader told me "You can have it all, you deserve it all." My "plan" had pictures of me enjoying the good life on the beach (I actually cut photos of me and pasted my face over the heads of the models in the magazines), earning $100,000 per month, public speaking, writing, travelling to Europe, delighting in family and friends, driving my new cars, living in several different homes of enormous value, helping out the less fortunate, jogging effortlessly in high fashion, and many affirmations all designed to remind me that I can achieve *these desires. I was told, at the workshop, that when I focus on my map every day I train my mind to do the things necessary to achieve these desires. As John Fowles said: "We are designed to want, with nothing to want we would be like windmills in the world without wind."*

Insight!

Focus, focus, focus!!

After several months I began to notice this "map" (pinned above my desk for easy contemplation and daydreaming) was confusing me on a conscious and perhaps even unconscious level. In which house did I want to live? Did I want to be a public speaker or an author, or an MLMer? There were various affirmations, none of them conflicting, but so many with different directions. Two cars, which one is mine? And so on.

FOCUS OR BUST??

Focus is one of the most important requirements of an MLMer, old or new. When I became aware of my confusion, I created a new treasure map that was more clearly focused. It has pictures and affirmations of me successfully writing and marketing this book. Simple, precise, direct. The book was completed and on the market within 120 days! Focus, focus, focus!

When you construct a "treasure map", or a list of affirmations, you are announcing to the universe that you desire something and that you *intend* to do something. First-hand experience has taught me that the universe is designed to give you whatever you want ("be careful of what you want, because you will get it"). When your request reaches the "Department of the Angels" for output, if they are confused, you will receive confusion. The challenge is to be very clear, focused, and unambiguous. Create several treasure maps throughout your life. As you achieve the essence of one, go on to another.

Belleruth Naparstek summarizes how important clear, unambiguous intention and desire are to each of us:

> *Whether stated aloud or in silence, in the form of words or images, clear intention is extremely important. Most of the people [successful] I interviewed were very conscious and deliberate about either giving voice to their intention or asserting it silently to themselves. Sometimes the intention would take the form of an image, projected in the mind's eye, or the process [achieving the goal] working well. Many had crafted a personal statement of their aims, which sometimes took the form of an affirmation or prayer that they used in a repeated, ritualized way to invoke their awareness. Whatever form it takes, intention is critical; it's the coherent force that shapes the energy of the field into the desired outcome. Nearly everyone I heard from emphasized the need to be clean and clear in their intention.*
>
> *(excerpted from Your Sixth Sense, by Belleruth Naparstek)*

You can have anything you want if you want it desperately enough. You must want it with an exuberance that erupts through the skin and joins the energy that created the world.
≥Sheila Graham

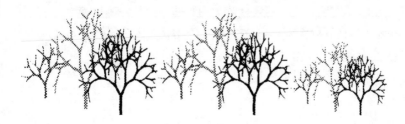

<u>April 10 - My first company convention - more confidence for the battle of Sisyphus. It was held in a high school gymnasium -- about 750 people from all over the country in attendance. It is very loud and electrifying, exciting, galvanizing, rousing - it was meant to be motivational -- and it was! The stories were impressive, some even made me cry and the sales training material was spectacular - I bought lots. I rubbed shoulders with my up up-line ($100,000 per month income) and felt 'if he can do it, so can I'. I was one of many to walk away with that "pumped up" feeling. As I sit here, a few days after the convention, and write about what I learned, I notice I don't feel as confident as when I walked out of the gym! Again I am reminded that external stimulation and motivation has a short shelf life.</u>

April 29 - During the last two weeks of April I spent some time calculating how I might climb to the next level (Silver) in my MLM. I know I can do it by the end of May. I have people working with me in my organization and I want SILVER!

May 15 - On May 1ˢᵗ I started prospecting everyone I know, every day of the week (being respectful and courteous of course!). it's the middle of the month & my sales volume is not half-way to what's required for the next pin level. Now What? I am weary and disappointed.

May 19 - Despair sets in for a few days. I lose focus and distract myself with old accounting business, putting MLM out of my mind.

May 20 - I am part way to my goal with ten more days left in the month - "just do it" becomes my daily slogan! More prospecting, coaxing friends to try my product and telling them about the business opportunity. These past few days have been good business-days. I'm selling more product and telling more people about my company and this new way of doing business - my spirits are high.

May 27 - Three days before the end of May and I'm $3,000 short of my objective. What to do? I call old clients and offer to buy back my product if they don't like it. On the last day of the month, close to the last hour, I qualify for a new pin level. What a race; what a rush; how exciting! Hope abounds, I am SILVER! Now, on to Gold!

Insight!

Perhaps when it's necessary for more than a few people to gather for training or information disbursement, the "leader" could provide a pot-luck atmosphere. It is well known that people are more comfortable in a casual environment where food is served. Learning of any sort is enhanced with play.

THE "OLD" MACHINE

MLM is supposed to represent a new way of doing business yet many still promote the old corporate model of suites, command and control, goals, business meetings, etc. It's as though we are reaching out for a new way to do commerce, yet since it is new, we are lacking the essential 'unique' tools for the job. So, we blend old with new. Let's think "outside the box" and when the old method presents itself, reject it – do something else. Be brazen and daring! This *is* creativity at its best.

A little history about where all this linear thinking came from might be helpful. Newtonian science was the father of cause and effect. It has dominated our society for more that two hundred years. We have structured our lives, organizations, and communities around this belief in command and control, cause and effect. This science allows us to believe one can pull a lever at one place and get a precise result at another, and know with certainty which lever to pull for which result; never mind that human beings must be made to perform like cogs and wheels in the process. We see this in our schools, our government, even our medical profession. By the way, rarely have we gotten the expected result!

For me, networking is a casual sport where there is little competition and great cooperation between you and your prospect and all the people in your organization. It's a business format that truly embraces a win-win situation with every human encounter. The command-and-control, cause-and-effect Newtonian philosophy seems like an oxymoron in relation to MLM. Why is it that we use old methods in this new model?

Even the basic training 'feels' like it comes from the philosophy of Peter Drucker or Edward Demming (two great business thinkers and leaders of the 20th century).

We are heading into the twenty-first century; we need new tools, new thinkers, new leaders. Networking from your heart (not your head or your fear of your next quarterly review) is the future of business, I'm convinced of it!

Looking your customer straight in the eye and silently telling her/him "I love you" *is* networking from your heart. That love-energy will be felt by your customer. What do you think it will do to the business encounter? Can you imagine the President of IBM silently telling the President of Boeing "I love you"? I wonder how the negotiations would turn out.

Today, as we leave behind the "old" machine, people want to know you before they buy or join your team. Frank P. Perdue, Chairman of the Board for Perdue Farms, Inc. has a clear vision of the future of network marketing. "Anonymous marketing just doesn't work anymore. Consumers want to know not only *what* they're buying, but *who* they're buying it from. The *people*, not the *logo*. Consumer relationship development is as important as product development."

Be a pioneer, assemble your SuccessLine frequently (schedule it!) to brainstorm about how the future might look. Think wild and crazy thoughts, create "The New Vehicle" not out of the past but into the future.

June 12 - With the help of some of my recruits, I started hosting my own public meetings this week. Why? Well, I saw that the high income earners contributed to the MLM community by offering a meeting place and bringing in other top earners as speakers. I have decided to imitate a few of the leaders as a way to climb to the Gold level. My organization is growing, albeit very slowly.

August 12 - The past 30 days have flown by quickly and my spirits are still high. The weekly meetings are a bit of a hassle; it seems like I just finish one and it's time for the next one. There is talk about someone higher up the ladder doing the meeting. I'm stirred by two emotions: relief and disappointment!?! I like the visibility I've gotten yet would like to get rid of the effort. I think my time can be better used by calling on customers, telling my story, and explaining about the business instead of always getting ready for the next lunch gathering.

October 31 - Well, summer has come and gone and I didn't achieve my goal of earning $10,000 per month! Why? Was summer too short a time-line? Perhaps I should have allowed more time. As the days turn cold I have less energy and hope for MLM. Yet, I still work at it every day and I receive a check every month. Why don't the people I meet see the future of MLM as clearly as I? Perhaps it's my vision that's cloudy. I decided to call Steve, the 'top-dog'. I figure since he's earning $250,000 per month, he must have some advice for me. Actually, I thought about making that call several weeks ago, but chickened out each time I looked at the phone. When I did call, he answered the phone himself - I was impressed - He said he had plenty of time for everyone in the organization. I told him about my efforts and my disappointments. He told me to take a walk, to clear my mind and soul, say a prayer and "start over"- just like it was my first day! That's it, this business is as simple as *talking to 2 new people a day about your company and products. Whenever your downline is not 'teaming' with you - start over and find other team players. I know I can do that!*

November 3 - I've started reading books and articles on success in business with an eye toward how to 'bridge' this information from the old model into the new paradigm. A 'group' of my colleagues and I formed a Master Mind weekly breakfast. We've decided to use Think and Grow Rich by Napoleon Hill as our workbook. Hill wrote this book in 1937, yet it contains timeless principles that we can adopt to MLM.

Insight!

We have been taught to put a time-line (could this be a limitation?) on achieving goals. It's been my personal experience that when that time comes and goes and the goal is unmet, disappointment sets in. So, I have taken time out of the equation. Trust the universe to support you . . . in its own correct timing.

GOALS

Goals and success: are they related, connected, necessary? The quick answer is yes, with a little twist. I believe, for example, that you can decide you want to earn $100,000 per month and achieve success. The success formula is presented below with my added torque:

1. Work backward to see what steps are required to achieve your goal. Your sponsor (in any MLM organization) should be happy to help you with this.
2. Write out the daily behavior necessary to achieve your goal. Affirmations, number of cold-calls or warm-calls, number of tapes in the mail, service to existing retail customers, and whatever else feels appropriate to your personal style.
3. Create visual aids (like a treasure map) that help you focus, focus, focus on your goal. Remember, you will call forth *precisely* what you think, feel, and say.
4. Remove the element of time from the equation.

I believe the universe will present to you that which you stay clear about, stay focused upon, and, most importantly, do not change your mind about. When you change your mind, you confuse the delivery system (the universe). When you make up your mind about something, you set the wheels in motion. Forces beyond you are engaged in a process that results in your desire. I believe in quantum cause and effect (for the physicists that might sound like an oxymoron), and I see a clear connection between goal setting, action plans, and results; however, the effects are not always immediate and/or apparent.

Consider that a small butterfly in Tokyo flapping its transparent wafer-thin wings will stir the air just enough that a chain of events, unbeknownst to the butterfly, will eventually swirl into a wind storm in southern Texas. The cause and effect is not apparent, yet none-the-less there is a complex connection.

Two people in my organization initially did nothing with the information I gave them. The cause was my telling them about my product and the business opportunity. The results came nine months later when one person needed the product for a client and the other wanted a new business opportunity.

November 10 - Last night I attended my weekly MLM meeting to hear one of the highest paid members speak. I've heard him before, but last night I learned something new. He tells the audience for the thousandth time, his story of how he got involved with this company. What I heard was his passion for MLM and his belief in our company & product. He tells his story every day . . . to someone new!

Insight!

Tell your story passionately, gently and often. Light many fires and develop an expectation that each person you talk with will join you (you never know how far your voice will travel). Read your goals every day, read your action plan every day, look at your visuals every day, imagine with all your senses what your goal feels like. Do this every day. Be aware of the joy in the journey and the rewards along the way, Stay clear, stay focused and above all, don't change your mind.

November 15 - I am amazed at how quickly my emotions are affected by this 'game' of MLM. Today I'm furious at my downline, upline and any & all I've tried to chase into this business! I'm especially disenchanted with my recruits. I can't seem to instill in them the same belief I have in networking as a career; Ugh! I feel better after having talked with Steve, two weeks ago. I do admire him and trust in his suggestion to start over! This stuff of being alone - on your own - seems a curse and a blessing! Just when you think someone understands and will "catch the vision", they drop out or say no!! The only source of inspiration is myself and those "masters" with whom I share moments via books and tapes. Now I understand how important it is to create an environment in which to feel confident of oneself!

November 20 - It's almost Giving Thanks Day and I have lots to be thankful for. A growing downline, increased retail sales, and more excitement each day for networking. A new, quiet feeling calms me. The other day at a business meeting I learned that more than half of the divorces in America could be avoided with just $250 to $300 more per month in income. Certainly a reasonable goal for a part-time MLMer. That makes me want to tell more people about MLM and how it can be done from the kitchen table - part time.

Insight!

The key to having distributors stay in your organization is to help them 'learn-to-earn' $300.00 per month as quickly as possible ~ about three to six months.

HELP THE MASSES?

When I got into MLM, I heard over and over how important it was to prospect the business-owner, the entrepreneur, the upper-end executive. The idea is to build a downline with "go-getters" - low maintenance distributors. Sounds great, yet the fact is MLM is populated with 1% go-getters and the rest part-time distributors happy to earn $300 or so per month. So, do I prospect for the one-percent or help the 99% achieve their goals? Ummm, I think I'll help the masses.

November 27 - I've just finished reading a book about achieving success by being authentic in all situations -- work, home, community. This insight is so inspiring that I feel like I did when I first started MLM 10 months ago. I'm always surprised at how learning something new can change how I "feel" as well as how bright the future appears. Am I still being manipulated by external motivation? Maybe, but I'm sure the insights I've just learned will take me one step (or perhaps two steps) closer to MLM-success. I am ready for Gold!

CONSULTING

Your work is to discover your work and then with
all your heart to give yourself to it.
                ≠Buddha

After about a year at this new way of marketing and business development, I realized I needed some tools to help my downline and help myself. I began reading about mentors and consulting.

I ran across *The Consultant's Calling* by Geoffrey M. Bellman, and started using some of his ideas in my MLM practice. What follows is mostly his work, re-worded to reach the ear of the serious network marketer. Geoff's concepts were gleaned through several years of working in and for corporate America (that very institution we MLMers feel might be tumbling down). I believe his research can be applied to our new paradigm – the MLM way of delivering goods and services.

My consulting and mentoring ideas come from a variety of, again, corporate sources such as trade magazines, journals, and business books. With MLM, one of the advantages is that the downline has direct contact with the 'successful leaders' and the resources of her/his upline at no cost! An informal research paper puts the value of all that 'upline consulting' at $1,000 to $1,500 per day! In the Mentoring chapter (pp. 63-70), I argue that you might consider waiving that free advice and actually look outside MLM for a mentor.

In *The Consultant's Calling*, Geoff tells the reader that the fundamental problem facing the consulting profession is that of integrity. It is my belief that this is also a potential problem facing the Network Marketing profession (I like calling it a profession, don't you?). The lack of integrity in MLM occurs when we take advantage of our 'prospects' by serving our own economic needs, rather than placing service to the prospect as the ***single-minded*** purpose of any and all contact!

What does that mean? The prospect (later to become your retail customer or perhaps a member of your organization) *is* the product! They will buy when and where they feel understood ("seek first to understand, then to be understood"). Our response to clients during the sales presentation is their best indication of how we will function under pressure, when it really counts. A serious business prospect should push us and test us. Our task is to stand firm, letting the person know who we are and what values and viewpoints we represent. Later we will talk about the importance of a mission statement, the clear understanding of who you are and what you believe. It is essential that you clearly know what you believe and intend. Standing firm and letting the client know who you are will come across loud and clear after you have written your mission statement.

The following is one of Geoff's questions/quotes that I have paraphrased for use in our MLM profession:

> *How do you thrive as a network marketer,*
> *contribute to the world, make friends, and*
> *become the person you want to be?*

In a way, this book is about answering that question. It's about responding to that little voice within each of us that calls us to journey toward the meaning of life. Since we spend a great deal of time working, perhaps some of the meaning in our lives can be achieved through what we do for a living. Perhaps it makes sense (does to me!) to put those networking hours to a higher motive than just the almighty dollar. Why not recognize our MLM work as an important path we are on, walking toward the meaning in our lives? That means everyday we could thrive, contribute, make new friends, and become our true and authentic selves – WOW!

I think of my current work as work I love to do, work I choose to devote myself to because of the special meaning it has for me. It is work that answers an internal call to inform, to teach. With this work I love to do, I experience each of the things Geoff addresses in his questions. Remember the words of Kahlil Gibran? He said, "Work is love made visible."

Why are you in MLM? Take the time now to answer that question, perhaps using Geoff's questions as a backdrop, then write the answer in your journal and read it out loud. If your answer is authentic and genuine, if it comes from your heart, it will pull you up when you're down in the dumps. It is my experience that when I don't know what I want or why I'm doing something, I am sentenced to doing what others want.

Would each day be more exciting to you if you knew that networking was a way of becoming yourself, a daily opportunity for self-discovery, rather than just a way of making a living? Would you awaken thrilled with the idea that today you'd learn more about *your* meaning of life?

I believe MLM presents you with an opportunity to get a glimpse of the answer to all those questions. It is a matter of perspective and keeping balance in our work so that we honor our life's purpose in our every MLM move. Being aware of this balance/perspective creates behaviors that are different from the actions we take when we honor work, authority, money, power, and tradition. It opens us to alternatives that are extraordinary.

How does one achieve this deeper awareness? Practice! Practice every day.

There are only four things to remember about the process of making your presentation, whether it be for the business opportunity or a potential sale or both – only four. Here they are:

1. Show up ~

I know this sounds silly and obvious, but in order to get the ball rolling you have to get to the meeting **on time**. Woody Allen said that "eighty percent of success is showing up." How do you dress? Be comfortable – whether it's a suit, or casual – and be 'you'. Remember MLM is about becoming who you are, so who are you? Shouldn't you figure out who you are before you go out and try to sell some of you and what you believe? Your first thoughts are not about how to package yourself, but about what your 'self' is. Sincerity, respect, love . . . all are qualities that lift each of us and they need to be shown, modeled, and cherished. When you make your 'self' the priority, marketing will fall into place on its on!

2. Be present ~

This is where I underline *so important!* Be with your prospect – be here and now, not in the future spending all the money you'll earn when this person joins your team, nor in the past wondering what your prospect from yesterday is going to do. Give this client all your attention, all of it. Be here and now. The following passage from *The Heart Aroused* by David Whyte, is for you to keep in mind during your next product demonstration: ". . . human kind never sees success as 'here', but always ahead, down the road." Perhaps success is indeed in the journey, not at the destination.

3. Tell the truth ~

The truth is out there -- and it will set you free! Don't exaggerate your product and its benefits and the financial rewards of your company. I regularly catch myself in some form of pretense. I am not proud of this, but it is the truth – my growing edge. I pretend to understand more about my profession than I really do. I act as if I have heard of a concept or a person I have never heard of. I sometimes nod my head as if I understand, when in fact, I don't. I pretend to be doing more work than I am really doing. I can also pretend to do less work than I actually am doing.

When my truth becomes unimportant I am in danger of losing my true self. MLM is brimming with the opportunity to 'stretch' the truth to get what you think you want. Avoid that temptation! Each time I 'distort' the truth a small but clear voice inside me says, "What you just said alters the truth and you know it!" These important internal messages keep me on track or at least close to track. Be aware of your little voice and stay on track. Afterall, that's where the train is running!

4. Don't be anxious about the results ~

This is a hard one. If you're anxious about the results, you may be tempted to leave the present and think about the future, which is unfair to your prospect. Remember to stay in the here and now. Make the presentation from your heart and be peaceful with the results. Easy words to type, hard concept to adhere to, 'eh? How do you do this? Practice. Give it a try. See and experience the outcome – you might like how it feels.

This chapter suggests that to thrive in MLM, make a contribution to the world, make friends (community), and become the person you want to be, it's important to pursue your work as a 'calling', bringing who you are to what you do – every day. For me, this is true.

You see, I live in the Pacific Northwest and I like the outdoors, so I often use the wilderness as a metaphor – like now for instance. Completing this chapter is like pausing on the trail with a heavy backpack. I am stepping off the trail to rest, reflect, and let others go by. Much like MLM, you will recruit a 'hot-shot' one day and while you're resting she/he will pass by you. It's okay. It isn't a race. It's about helping others get what they want, all the while receiving what you need.

The following seven points summarize Geoff's book. I couldn't improve on 'em so here they are just as he published them but with references to MLM instead of consulting:

1. Find work you love to do and are called to do.
2. If Network Marketing is not your calling, then get out of it. Life is too short to spend all those hours on work you do not want to do.
3. When your work is your calling, where you are going is even more exciting than where you have been – and it *is* riskier, even a bit frightening.
4. There is no magic way to Network. There is no "only" way, no best way, no right way. You will choose your own way.
5. Pay attention to yourself and you will find that you know what to do next. Your experience, awareness, intuition, and common sense combine to tell you what to do. The task is getting everything else out of the way so that you know what you want to do.
6. You will never "arrive"; you will never be the complete MLMer. Others may think you have arrived yet you will know you have not. There is always more to become . . . no destination worth reaching and settling down into forever.
7. Doing this work without love is unfulfilling. Separating love and your work is unnatural. Together they bring fulfillment.

In order that people may be happy in their work, these three things are needed: They must be fit for it. They must not do too much of it. And they must have a sense of success in it.

✍John Ruskin

December 12 - Early in the morning, just before sunrise, the world is very still and very quiet. This morning it's especially silent because of the new fallen snow covering my home. I feel like I'm wrapped in a blanket and protected from the "cold" harsh world - funny, eh? As I sit and write, a melancholy feeling saturates my soul. I am wishing I could talk with someone about my MLM frustrations; someone other than my upline. It's almost like I could use a therapist or counselor - but that's not quite what I mean, perhaps a coach or mentor not affiliated with my MLM would be helpful. Someone not invested in why I'm asking questions or what the outcome is.

Insight!

Hire a professional coach or mentor outside your MLM organization.

MENTORING

The truth is that in many upline situations the ability to properly act as a mentor is missing. That statement is not meant to diminish anyone anywhere in MLM. After more that a year in Networking I am only reporting what I have observed and experienced. Many top producers get to the top without really knowing or understanding how it happened. Consequently, they are unable to give you practical, 'how-to' advice.

If you are going to treat this as a business and succeed the way franchisers have, then you will need to be trained and coached. The bottom line is you may have to pay for that training.

Mentorship is a process whereby the mentor and a protégé work collaboratively toward the goal of promoting and developing the protégé's abilities, knowledge and thinking skills. These two people enter into a kind of partnership which is actually reciprocal in nature (the teacher is student and student is teacher). The teacher and student have different learning goals. They each look for someone who challenges them and continues to help them grow and learn.

Being an effective mentor requires more than offering professional advice and guidance. It means having a big card file and the willingness to share who you know with your protégé − having enough confidence in your student to introduce him/her to your circle of influence. It might be difficult finding such a person within your MLM upline structure, wouldn't you agree? Additionally, a mentor probably would only want to work with a few protégés at a time. Come to think of it, the protégé would probably appreciate that ratio also.

One essential piece of the mentoring relationship is a written learning contract. This document, negotiated individually between each mentor-protégé team, requires that the protégé provide information similar to the following:

- What results will I produce in my MLM organization during the six months I will be working with my mentor?
- What habits and obstacles, in behavior and circumstances, will I have to overcome in order to achieve my stated goals in this six month period?
- What type of help do I want my mentor to provide? Assessing MLM prospects? Investigating how well presentations are received? Feedback on my observations about advertising, prospecting, and recruiting opportunities? Something else?
- How can my mentor help me overcome the obstacles that make it difficult to achieve my goals over this six month period?
- Finally, list any other agreements, commitments or conditions negotiated by you and your mentor that will apply to your work together over the next six months.

The mentoring 'clock' does not start until both agree to the terms of the learning contract, but the learning itself *begins* with this negotiation process. *Getting expectations and perceptions down in writing results in clarity and direction.* After the contract is signed, the pair will schedule regular meetings to discuss developmental goals, issues and progress. Accountability sets in and, as they say at the race track, "they're off!"

Does the help of a mentor make a difference in the effectiveness of an individual's performance? The evidence suggests it does. In one study of 22 executives, six "success factors" were identified. The only factor cited by all twenty-two executives was "Help from Mentor".

I am suggesting that the serious Business Networker look outside the organization for mentor help. I am also very clear that your upline - downline - crossline (I call these directions my SuccessLine) can provide excellent advice. So, don't abandon them; instead, why not have a mentor-protégé relationship both inside and outside your MLM organization?

Often people attempt to live their lives backwards; they try to have more things, or more money, in order to do more of what they want so that they will be happier. The way it actually works is the reverse. You must first be who you really are, then, do what you need to do in order to have what you want.

✍ Margaret Young

January 24 -My one year anniversary -- WOW, one year in the MLM business and boy have I learned a lot about who I am and what I want out of life. It's obvious at this point that I still have much work to do to get clear about what I want and who I am, but I'm proud and happy at the progress I've made to date. I read a sub-title on a book cover the other day that keeps surfacing in my consciousness -- "If you knew who you were, you could be who you are!" MLM is giving me the opportunity to discover who I am! My biggest learning thus far has been to keep my eye on the goal up ahead all the while enjoying each step along the path. I don't do it every day -but often enough so that I see some headway. Afterall, it is possible I won't get to that goal, so it's imperative that I live this moment fully. I have strengthened my resolve and renewed my desire to succeed in MLM.

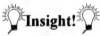

Insight!

If you know who you were, you can be who you are!

A man is not successful because he hasn't failed. Man is a success because he doesn't let failure stop him.
⮑Analects of K'ung Chiu,
500 BC

ENTREPRENEUR, KNOW THYSELF!

In the opening of her book, *A Passion for the Possible,* Jean Houston asks a question that is 'right-on' for Network Marketers. "What is it that enables some people to tap into their creative power and achieve remarkable things in music, art, literature, and science, while others flounder in despair and confusion, cut off from the artist and creator within?" Good question, don't you agree? Of course by now you have probably figured out that I believe everything we do as humans is creative and tinged by the artist within each of us. As I trek along this MLM road I believe I've found part of the answer to Houston's question.

One of the main things that distinguishes the highly successful MLMer from those who don't do as well is that the triumphant ones have confidence that their failures strengthen them to keep going. They have learned to tap into *their* creative power and use the experience to 'self-correct' if defeat occurs. I have taken Jean Houston's question and focused it at Network Marketing: Why is that 97 out of 100 people who enter MLM never reach their goals?

Perhaps having a clear picture of 'self' will increase your odds of MLM success. If you have already ventured out on your own or have a burning desire to be an entrepreneur, then this chapter is written for you. It has been created to help you identify your strengths and unique capabilities. It is my intention that this section assist you in more clearly understanding your unique entrepreneurial style and temperament.

71

This is not a "what to do" chapter; rather it is about "what to be," which is, of course, the very best you possibly can. I will not repeat time-worn concepts such as goal setting, strategy formulation, and tactical maneuvering; instead, I will address the unique modus operandi of the MLM entrepreneur and discuss how different styles ultimately determine what kind of entrepreneur you are, or you are likely, to become.

The playwright George Bernard Shaw wrote, "The reasonable man adapts himself to the world. The unreasonable one persists in trying to adapt the world to himself. Therefore, all progress depends on the unreasonable man." This is not to suggest that all entrepreneurs are unreasonable. It is to point out that inherent in the entrepreneurial process is the ability to identify, honor, and live with diversity as a normal, everyday process. Sounds like MLM, 'eh?

Entrepreneurs who are able to sustain their momentum know the road to success is *always* under construction. They leave the impression of forever arriving yet never quite reaching their goal. Stop for a moment and think about the successful MLMers you know. Are they forever pushing their goals out to a new horizon? Are they always reaching for the next challenge? Do you think of them as in a constant state of transition in which the journey is the goal? Moreover, do they really want to arrive? If they do, then it is all over and what do they do next?

This attempt to "know thy self" is as much about your prospects, as it is about you, the entrepreneur. To illustrate this, I'm going to share with you a bit of information about two personality profiles. In the old paradigm they were called 'instruments' and used by the Human Resource Department. I have figured out how to adapt these Newtonian devices to our needs. These two tools could become invaluable in your search to know more about both you and your prospects/team players!

One personality indicator measures your proclivity for success; based on your personal ability to cope with crises (on the way to or away from mastery). The other gauges how you take in information, sort it, and then make decisions.

Would it be helpful to understand your unique type of entrepreneurship? I believe this information can reduce your risk of failure and even help focus your energy on those tasks and behaviors where you are likely to perform at your best. There are many opportunities for success. Perhaps your strength lies in making presentations to groups, or perhaps it lies in giving one-on-one demonstrations, or in explaining the numbers vs. giving your prospect the big picture, etc. The point is to learn where to spend your time as well as how to help those in your organization spend their time and effort wisely. This way everyone prospers.

I found the first tool while reading *Adversity Quotient - Turning Obstacles into Opportunities* by Paul G. Stoltz. Dr. Stoltz asserts that his discovery is more significant than Intelligent Quotient (IQ), education, or social skills. He says in his introduction, "Your Adversity Quotient (AQ) measures your ability to prevail in the face of adversity." Look around you. How many MLM companies have top earners missing one or more of the qualities Stoltz listed? Because MLM doesn't require a high IQ, an advanced education, or even great manners or social skills, I believe it is a level playing field. Anyone with a high Adversity Quotient can make MLM a successful part of their lives. Don't panic . . . Stoltz actually teaches you how to increase your AQ.

We will also look at a methodology which comes from the Swiss psychologist, Carl Gustav Jung. In the 1950's two American women, Katharine C. Briggs and her daughter Isabel Briggs-Myers, put into questionnaire form, Jung's concepts about the differences and preferences within and between the human family. Today this profile is so well accepted that in the last year 2,500,000 people completed the questionnaire. The validated results were used to help people find new careers, learn to communicate better with their spouses and co-workers, decide which college to attend . . .the list is limited only by your imagination. You can use the Myers-Briggs Profile to get a handle on how you might proceed in network marketing and it can be very important in recruiting.

ADVERSITY QUOTIENTS

Adversity introduces a [person] to themselves.
✍Anonymous

Let's look first at your Adversity Quotient. In his book, Stoltz compares professional success to a steep mountain that must be climbed: "Fulfillment [in your professional and personal life] is achieved by relentless dedication to the ascent, sometimes slow, painful step, by slow, painful step." When I read those words I immediately thought of network marketing!

How many times have you heard "the only way to fail in MLM is to quit?" Stoltz goes on to say, "Scaling the mountain is an indescribable experience, one only the fellow climbers can understand and share." I remember the feeling of joy and accomplishment when my organization created enough volume to ratchet me up to the next pin-level. Oh, what a glorious day that was! If you haven't made the climb, be it mountain or MLM, you can't really imagine the feeling. Amid the relief, satisfaction, and exhaustion is a sense of joy and peace as rarefied as the mountain air. Only the Climber tastes this sweet success. Those who stay encamped may be justified, as well as warmer and safer, but never will they feel "on purpose," as alive, as proud and as joyful.

Success can be defined as the degree to which one moves forward and upward, progressing in one's lifelong mission, despite all obstacles or other forms of adversity. Stoltz and many others who have studied human behavior and potential agree that humans are born with a drive to soar with the eagles.

Is there perhaps a question on your mind at this point? If we all have this built-in drive to soar, achieve, and ascend, why then is the mountaintop not overcrowded and the base unpopulated? Looking around at the world, it seems to be the reverse.

To answer this question, Stoltz examined what occurs in three types of people whom we encounter along our journey up the mountain, or on our way to the top of our MLM.

The Quitter

Quitters refuse to take on the challenge of climbing the mountain. These people choose to sit on their hands, ignoring their potential in an attempt to avoid the hardship of the climb, evading both risk of failure and success. They basically drop out! They reject the chance that life presents to them. With great effort, they deny their human drive to soar and miss out on much of what life offers. The Network Marketing industry sidelines are populated with these potential soaring souls. Stoltz has a method to teach these people how to get back into the game, read on!

The Camper

These people go only so far, and then say, "this is it – I can't (or won't) go any farther!" Weary of the climb, they stop the quest to soar. They find a comfortable place to live out the rest of their life and thereby hide from adversity. In exchange for their comfort it appears that they give up excitement, learning, growth and higher achievements. In their favor it must be mentioned that they at least took on the challenge, albeit they did not finish.

This next piece is important, so listen up.

The camper did reach a certain place on the mountain and some view this as "success" in the final, conclusive sense of the word. Here's the important part - it's not the destination but the journey that defines success. Although Campers may have been successful in reaching the campground, they cannot maintain success without continuing to climb. I believe it is the lifelong growth and improvement of one's self that defines the climb.

The Climber

The people who are dedicated to the lifelong ascent are referred to as the Climbers. Regardless of education, IQ, social standing, money, good luck, bad luck, etc., these people *always* continue to climb. Their motto might be "things turn out best for those who make the best out of the way things turn out." They are like the batteries in that forever-running big pink bunny. Climbers are possibility thinkers, never allowing age, gender, race, physical or mental disability, or any other obstacle to get in the way of their climb. Climbers feel a deep sense of purpose and passion for what they do. They are the self-motivated, highly driven individuals who make things happen. Sound like entrepreneurs? Any high level MLMers come to mind?

The discipline and validity of AQ is built on more than 35 years of research by dozens of top scholars and more than 1,000 studies from around the world. It draws on breakthroughs in three major sciences: cognitive psychology, psycho-neuroimmunology, and neurophysiology (the science of the brain).

77

March 12 I took the AQ test and scored a moderate climber. While writing "Confessions" it occurred to me that I had not been on a real mountain climb in several years. If presented with the opportunity, would I quit, camp, or climb I wondered? So, I created the opportunity. Today, I closed down my computer and chose a climb that was a bit out of reach for my age (two-score and 9). I was intent on enjoying the journey, all the while keeping my eye on the top of the mountain.

The trailhead presented me with a feeling of excitement (similar to the beginning days in MLM) and the knowledge that the climb ahead was going to take persistence. The first thing I noticed was a pack of children, one as young as four years, running up the trail asking dad how far to the top. They were on a leisurely family-hike using the same trail I had chosen to test my mettle. Ummm, perhaps there's something to learn here about perspective. The children reminded me of the Stoltz premise that we are born with the drive to succeed, to soar, to ascend- they sure were!.

Thirty minutes into the hike I was aware my feet hurt -"maybe this isn't such a good idea" I thought. After all it's just a hike, it's not the end of the world if I quit and go home. Quit? No way! This trek is a metaphor for my life. I must stand at the top and claim victory. I could feel the backpack straps cutting into my shoulders - it hurt. Next time I'll plan better, carry less weight perhaps, or spend time getting in better physical shape. MLM is about planning and being in shape; mentally, physically, spiritually. ... such parallels.

Sometimes I was alone on the trail. What a fine feeling, having only the trail, trees, a few birds, and the sound of the water all to myself. I enjoyed the solitude. Then, suddenly I had companions on the trail again and that too felt wonderful. To stop the ascent for a few minutes of human-ness, sharing information about the trail up-

ahead and behind, listening to the excited accounts of the effort seemed to urge me on, encourage me to continue. There is a human need for community along the journey, people to help and receive help from, stories to tell, opportunities to seize. I am reminded of a saying I heard recently "we tell stories because that is how we know who we are."

On my climb, I encountered a young man with long golden hair, tied in a ponytail. He was wearing a pewter earring of Kokopelli, the god of fertility. Strangely (or was it synchronicity?) I too was wearing Kokopelli (around my neck) and immediately felt a bond with the stranger. We talked of the climb and it's challenges and rewards and, because he had already made the ascent, he helped me by sharing tips he'd discovered along the path. "Be careful of the wooden bridge over Cold Creek, it's support beams are rotting away", he cautioned me.

Seems to me that if we are going to help those who come into our MLM biz after us, we need to have experienced the climb. I've learned that practical advice about where to step and not to step comes from personal knowledge. it's clear to me now after 18 months that only after you've stood at the top, endured the challenge, can you talk about it with any authority. With your own words, you will convey your energy and enthusiasm and it will be contagious! Your personal experience will influence any and all you encounter along the path. MLM is an experiential business; you have to 'do-it' before you can teach it!

It was the first operatic mountain I climbed, and the view from it was astounding, exhilarating, stupefying.

✐Leontyne Price

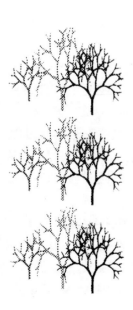

March 13 - I am pleased I took the challenge to climb yesterday - I did make it to the top - what a great feeling it was. Taking off my backpack and my shoes, sitting in the sun with my feet in the water was enough reward for taking the risk. It was hard work and exhilarating. The chemicals in my body mixed a concoction that created a feeling of euphoria within me. There is a special excitement that comes with pouring ourselves completely into an especially important project. I love to do that! I come out on the other side exhausted and, I hope, successful. Sitting on that mountain top brought back memories of the day I climbed up to the next financial level in my MLM. There was a feeling of joy, accomplishment, excitement, exhaustion and great hope.

Surprisingly (recalling my descent off the mountain), I feel happy; no, it is more like contentment, or satisfaction. I would think the 'coming down' might feel empty. After all, the goal and subsequent victory was getting to the top -- wasn't it? No? I'm learning that the victory is the journey. I'm back in my office again -- missing the mountain a bit.

Insight!

The news is good!

The many people who have learned to give up when adversity strikes, can retrain themselves to keep going, by increasing their AQ!

Let's take a look at the three components of AQ and then see how this might help us in our MLM organization.

From the first building block of AQ, cognitive psychology, we learn that people respond to adversity in subconscious, *consistent patterns that remain stable throughout their lives unless something is done to change them.* Researchers have found that how people respond to adversity is a strong predictor of success. WOW! Wouldn't you like to have a sense of how successful your SuccessLine will be?

From the second building block, psychoneuroimmunology, we learn that there is a direct link between response to adversity and physical and mental health. Numerous studies have established that poor responses to adversity can lower immune functions, decrease the chances of recovery from surgery, and increase one's vulnerability to life-threatening diseases. When people respond to adversity with a sense of personal responsibility, they live longer. Does any part of our society support this sense of personal control? I believe it's unusual to find an institution that teaches us about our personal power, our personal authority. From schools to jobs, to government, we are often made to believe we are ultimately out of control. Perhaps this is one reason why there are only 1% to 3% at the top of MLM.

And finally, from the third building block of AQ, neurophysiology, we learn that the brain has an amazing ability to take repeated thoughts or behaviors and hardwire them into *subconscious habits.* When first learning to do something, you are very aware of what you are doing; you have to concentrate on the activity. With repetition, a destructive thought or action (such as a poor response to adversity) becomes subconscious and automatic.

The good news is that self-defeating habits can be interrupted and changed in an instant (see holographic re-patterning information on page 93). For example, when you touch a hot stove, a loud alarm sounds in your brain that interrupts the thought patterns in the subconscious part of your brain, bringing the sound of alarm to your conscious mind. In the same way, an unproductive response to adversity can be brought to your conscious mind and replaced with a better one. Through repetition, one can re-wire old negative patterns into new positive habits.

In a five-year study of insurance agents (self-employed just like MLM distributors), Metropolitan Life hired a sales force of high AQ applicants based solely on their responses to Stoltz' Adversity Quotient Questionnaire. Because the agents did *not* match the traditional success profile, they would not have been recruited under normal circumstances – yet this group became the company's top producers. Knowing a person's AQ allows one to predict who will overcome obstacles, and who may not!

Are you ready for a bit of good news? No matter where you score on the continuum (quitter to climber), you can improve your Adversity Quotient! Stoltz has developed a series of exercises to improve AQ in yourself, others, and your organization. It can happen quickly; in a matter of a few weeks. After asking you to complete the questionnaire and calculate your AQ, Stoltz takes you through a well-tested technique designed to help transform destructive responses to life's events.

He calls his system LEAD. You can use the LEAD sequence in two ways: first, as a tool for strengthening your own AQ; second, as a valuable leadership tool for helping others to move from complaints to solutions. It goes beyond listening by guiding the individual to action, while avoiding the typical trap of giving advice.

LEAD is an acronym made up of the first letters of the four techniques that follow:
1. **L**isten to your adversity response. Was it a high or low response?
2. **E**xplore all origins of the adversity response and your ownership of the result.
3. **A**nalyze the evidence.
4. **D**o something.

Each of the above steps are integrated into the five dimensions of Control, Origin, Ownership, Reaching, and Endurance. I am not going to dive any deeper into this subject now, except to urge you to get your hands on his book and start the process. It's fun, enlightening and may be profitable. Maybe you could invite your front line to work through the book as a team, using a master mind group format?

Nothing in the world can take the place of Persistence. Talent will not; nothing is more commonplace than unsuccessful [people] with talent. Genius will not, unrewarded genius is almost a proverb. Education alone will not, the world is full of educated derelicts. Persistence and Determination alone are omnipotent.

✍Calvin Coolidge

3/15 -- Beware the Ides of March. Spring is in the air - although the nights are still cold and the days still wet I can smell new growth. In my quest to learn all that I can about myself I have made an appointment to undergo a new way to change an old habit. I quietly admit to myself and this journal the possibility that I own destructive habits that I cannot consciously change AND, perhaps they keep me from experiencing all my MLM goals. The anticipation is scary and exciting and exhilarating. Doing something new for the first time has always been a challenge for me -- so "leap and the net will appear" is my motto.

Insight!

Taking action *'outside the box'* is a challenge and yet, for many, essential for personal growth.

HOLOGRAPHS AND YOU??

Let's have a little fun by stepping out onto the fringe (or the frontier, if you choose) and looking at an alternative to traditional habit-changing methodology. While reading and subsequently experiencing the Stoltz material, I discovered another procedure designed to help change old habitual patterns. Stoltz' techniques change behavior through awareness and rewiring the neuro-pathways by using repetition. Holographic Repatterning, on the other hand, can change behavior at the cellular or energetic level, sometimes within an hour! I'm not kidding!

I must admit, I have been known to haunt psychic fairs and other new-age gatherings in my quest to learn. At one such fair I sat in on a lecture given by a professional Medical Intuitive – one who assesses energetic fields in an attempt to bring clients into the present time, wherein all healing occurs. I was impressed with the presentation and motivated to try the kind of "healing work" offered. This energy work changed a habit I've been working on for several years. The shift was subtle and yet obvious! In a 90-minute session my inclination to procrastinate was noticeably reduced. *(Evidence: this book is in your hands and not still in my head.)*

What Holographic Repatterning does is shift the energy and resonance behind belief systems, thereby, shifting perceptions and experiences. This shift can be prompted in many ways - through sound, essences, color and other such healing modalities. The Repatterning process uses a variety of these healing modalities to assist the shifting process ~ it's fun, unique, experiential, and dare I say it again, effective. It uses the inborn wisdom of your Body-Mind System to move a belief system that has locked you into a particular habit. The process gives you a fresh view of what you are doing and the *choices* you are making so that you begin to "see" the stage-play that is going on. You know, the theater in which you participate daily! You can still choose to make old familiar choices, but somehow Holographic Repatterning clears obstacles for more optimal choices, if (using free will) we so desire.

Want more good news? When you shift energetically, you don't have to keep going back and reminding yourself to make different choices, e.g. with affirmations. You have shifted an innate piece of your Being, your energetic pattern, that energetic grid that identifies you as *you*! Don't misunderstand me, daily affirmations are important, yet they can only get you so far. If your belief system is in conflict with that affirmation, there is no way you will talk yourself out of a negative pattern. That's because the habit pattern is an energy with which you resonate at your core level.

So there you have it. Two ways to change a habit that may be new to you. One, scientific and the other new scientific.

> *Changing a habit or a belief at an energetic level is the most viable and effective mode available for self-transformation.*
>   ✍ Jo Chaves [*]

---

[*] Jo Chaves, Medical Intuitive - Kirkland, Washington (425) 820-5934

MYERS-BRIGGS TYPE INDICATOR

You're probably asking: why do I want to be aware of my unique psychological type? Don't quit. Keep <u>Climbing</u>! I promise I'll make it fun and useful – I promise.

Psychological type provides a framework for working with the personality differences you encounter everyday. It is the basis for increased understanding of yourself and more effective dealings with all people whether friends, family, or MLMers. The next time you sit with a new MLM prospect at a 'coffee-shop' presentation, you can observe his/her behavior and modify your course of action to accommodate his/her "stuff" (**if** you have an understanding of what we affectionately call MBTI®). For example, there are folks who think "out loud", so just listen if you want to know what's on their mind. Another 'type' thinks quietly, so you have to ask, "what are you thinking?" and then – here's the hard part for some of us – after you ask the question, be quiet! Wait for an answer.

The theory of psychological typing was developed by Carl Jung (Swiss psychiatrist born in 1875) to explain some of the seemingly random differences in people's behavior. From his research of clients and others, Jung found predictable and differing patterns of normal behavior. His theory of psychological type looks at these patterns, or types, and provides an explanation of how each develops.

In the 1940's two women, Katharine Briggs and Isabel Myers, designed a self-report questionnaire, the *Myers-Briggs Type Indicator®* (MBTI®) to make Jung's theory understandable and useful in every day life (e.g. in your MLM organization).

This theory has been proven to a high degree of reliability over the past 50 years and predictable differences in individuals seem to show up in the way people prefer to use their minds. When your mind is active, you are involved in one of two mental activities:

- taking in information *(Perceiving)*
- organizing information and coming to conclusions *(Judging)*

Jung observed that there are two opposite ways to perceive, which he called *Sensing* and *Intuition*, and two opposite ways to judge, which he called *Thinking* and *Feeling*.

Okay, time out! So what? How's this going to help me with my MLM business, you ask? Hang in for two more short paragraphs and I'll knit it together for you.

Different people prefer to focus their energy in different ways, either toward the external world or toward the internal world. The preference for the external world of people, things, and experiences is known as *Extroversion* and the preference for the internal world of inner processes and reflections is *Introversion*. Myers and Briggs, when constructing the MBTI® profile, said that each individual prefers to handle the world around them in either a way that moves to closure *(Judging)* or a way that stays open to suggestion *(Perceiving)*. These four basic dimensions give you eight ways of using your mind. Jung taught that all people have these same eight choices.

Here comes the practical part. The eight dimensions (choices, if you prefer) are organized on four scales, each consisting of two opposite poles. The MBTI® indicates your unique preferences by your questionnaire score on each scale. For example, either you prefer to receive "hard data" or you use your "intuition" to make decisions. Your score will place you at one-end or the other on the *Sensing - Intuition* scale.

Below is a brief description and a few characteristics of each dimension:

1. Where you prefer to focus attention:
    *   Extroversion people find they often prefer to bounce ideas off others and *talk it out.*
    *   Introversion people find they work best if they can build in plenty of quiet time to *think it through - alone.*
2. How you prefer to assimilate information:
    *   Sensing people find they trust and pay attention to *specifics.* They want a lot of hard data – give them the whole enchilada, audio tapes, video tapes of your business opportunity, all the information you can dig up on your product, etc.
    *   Intuition people need the *big picture* – tell them about the *possibilities,* about how the product helps others, etc.
3. How you prefer to make decisions (after assimilating the information):
    *   Thinking people often base their decisions on *logical implications.* They use cause-and-

effect reasoning, and are often the "tough-minded" executives who make impersonal and objective decisions.

- Feeling people often base their decisions on the *impact on other people.* They are guided by personal values, they strive for harmony and individual validation, they are the "tender-hearted".

4. How you align yourself to the external world:

- Judging people often like to "wrap it up"– they like *closure.* They are methodical, systematic, and highly organized.
- Perceiving people usually make *"no decision before it's time"* – they like the process *of processing.* They are spontaneous, casual, flexible and feel energized by last-minute pressures (like getting this book to the publisher by tomorrow!).

This is not Hollywood! No Type Casting Allowed!

Everyone uses each of the eight processes, but **prefers** one in each of the four dimensions. This means that when you are free to choose an activity *without* outside demands, you use an approach that is "natural" for you. It may simply *feel* easiest or it may be "how you always start." It is important to remember that this information is NOT to be used to "type" yourself or your customers. It's not for manipulation, it is for information.

Eventually, with practice, you will be able to use your NON-preferred style in the selling cycle in order to give your customer what she/he wants. As a salesperson (yes, it's sales in MLM), you are not going to know the psychological type preference of your customers. You do not need to. In fact, although every prospect will show a fairly stable set of cues, many will move through all of the eight preferences while they are working with you. This is especially true if the buying decision is a significant one (like joining your MLM team). It is likely you will already have noticed how a particular prospect usually interacts with you. You may also note when her/his behavior changes. These changes may actually be disconcerting to you. You may wonder what you did or what you *should* do next. Using the MBTI®, you can better understand the differences in your client's behavior, tolerate changes when they occur, and adapt your approach as needed. The world needs a bit more sensitivity and tolerance, so why not start here?

It is meaningful, when using a personality type framework to understand the following points:

- Differences between people are natural, not something you can change or would want to change.
- All type *preferences* are positive, no aspect of any preference is better or worse than another.
- Other's preferences may be directly *opposite* your natural preference . . . here's another chance to bend and seek to understand.
- Some behaviors have nothing to do with type preference.

Adapting to a prospect is very important. It puts the person at ease and gives them space in which to make an informed and comfortable decision. You want new recruits to be in your organization by their choice (remember "if you drag 'em in - you'll have to drag them around").

Several studies indicate that "dislike of the salesperson" is the most significant reason for not buying a service or product. I'm convinced that you can help others be at ease with diversity and improve the image of the 'disliked salesperson' by getting clear about your "type" at the same time learning how to use your non-preferred type in the right setting.

Keep in mind that using this tool in selling is a discipline. As you begin using it, you will have immediate payoff in terms of more understanding and control in the selling situation. As you continue to work with it you gain fluidity, ease, and an ever greater appreciation of your 'self', your customers, your family and diversity.

A few comments about the MBTI® questionnaire and then we'll move on to developing your very own personal mission statement (just like a real company). The questionnaire takes about 45 minutes to complete and perhaps 2-3 hours to validate and interpret. The *validation process is critical* In order for you to get a handle on your unique *preferences* in life, it is long-term important that you complete the MBTI® accurately. Verifying your four attitudes takes about an hour; it's fun, and helpful to you and your organization. Again, I suggest you consider putting together a workshop with your top leaders (or those you want to become your top leaders) and bring in a qualified MBTI® trainer for a half-day program. There are MBTI® practitioners in every state and in several countries - look in your local phone book or give me a call.

A final word about 'typing' and your future. I know people who after completing the MBTI® and writing their mission statement (next chapter), leave MLM. Yes, it's true. Some people don't belong in Network Marketing and after these chapters they simply get 'clear' and pursue their life's dream. It's okay! Part of why I wrote this book was to help you see why you're in MLM and help you decide whether you should stay.

April 15 - Tax Day! Being a Tax-Accountant for 23 years, I remember dreading this day - physically, mentally, and emotionally worn - frazzled to the bone. No more, thanks to MLM. I have a confession. Last year when I attended the weekend training, one of the exercises was creating mission statement. I didn't do it because I didn't think it was important. WRONG! Boy was I wrong. As I look back over the past 15 months, I see several forks in the road where, since I didn't have a clear idea of my mission, I did what Yogi Berra suggested -- "When you come to a fork in the road, take it." I haven't always taken the correct fork because I didn't know my mission. "The mystery is: here is the fork in the road, but which way is up?" Perhaps I shall begin again and create my personal mission statement - YES!

Insight

Mission statement work is the single most important work because the decisions made there affect all other decisions. ✍Dr. Stephen R. Covey

MISSION STATEMENTS

A mission statement . . . I must admit I wish I could think of a better name for it - no matter, it is the beginning of personal and organizational leadership. It provides overall direction and clarifies your purpose and meaning. By referring to it, and internalizing its meaning, you are more likely to choose behavior that serves your values and reject behavior that opposes them. In other words, you will filter your major decisions through your mission statement - if it fits, great! If not; don't do it!

Mission statements are considered so vital to the life and the survival of an organization that major companies spend hundreds of thousands of dollars and significant time (months and years) developing them. Don't underrate the impact of your own personal mission statement. I would venture a guess that all (yes all) successful MLMers have a company or personal mission statement. It's probably printed on the back of their business card, or in their purse/wallet for easy reading. They read it every day and base each decision on it. It's consequential; it's part of the success formula I=R (Intention equals Results).

Laurie Beth Jones, in her book *The Path* puts the need for a mission statement into perspective: "In a world in which we are daily forced to make decisions that lead us either closer to or further from our goals, no tool is as valuable in providing direction as a mission statement -- a brief, succinct [no more than one sentence according to Ms. Jones], and focused statement of purpose that can be used to initiate, evaluate, and refine all of life's activities. A carefully thought out mission statement acts as both a harness and a sword -- harnessing you to what is true about your life, and cutting away all that is false."

In MLM, it is my experience that distributors are presented daily with dozens of decisions; the proverbial "forks in the road". With a mission statement in your hand and in your heart, you will be able to decide which road to take in order to achieve objectives – harness and cut away as needed.

Let's look at a few well known company statements before we get in any deeper.

Microsoft Corporation --

> *A computer on every desk and in every home.* (Statements don't have to be long and wordy, that's the good news.)

Southwest Airlines --

> *The mission of Southwest Airlines is dedication to the highest quality of Customer Service delivered with a sense of warmth, friendliness, individual pride, and Company Spirit.* (A little longer but still not daunting.)

Ben & Jerry Ice Cream --

> *Ben & Jerry's is dedicated to the creation and demonstration of a new corporate concept of linked prosperity* (sounds like MLM, eh?). *Our mission consists of three interrelated parts:*
>
> > Product Mission: *To make, distribute and sell the finest quality all-natural ice cream and related products in a wide variety of innovative flavors made from Vermont dairy products.*
> >
> > Social Mission: *To operate the company in a way that actively recognizes the central role that business plays in the structure of society by initiating innovative ways to improve the quality of life of a broad community; local, national, and international.*

> Economic Mission: *To operate the company on a sound financial basis of profitable growth, increasing value for our shareholders and creating career opportunities and financial rewards for our employees.*
>
> (Underlying the mission of Ben & Jerry's is the determination to seek new and creative ways of addressing all three parts, while holding a deep respect for individuals, inside and outside the company, and for the community of which they are a part.)

In the 1960's, when Gene Roddenberry wrote the TV series *Star Trek*, he also authored a mission statement that would become familiar to millions.

> *Space, the Final Frontier ... These are the voyages of the Starship Enterprise. Its Five-year Mission: To explore strange new worlds, to seek out new life and new civilizations, to boldly go where no man has gone before."*

Ultimately, whenever and wherever people gather and attempt to achieve something purposeful, they pronounce a mission or purpose to everyone participating; to all the stakeholders as corporate America puts it. Thinking of a mission statement as part of a company's overall blueprint for success and communicating that to all involved gives a company a head start on achieving that success. That's exactly how it should work for you and your SuccessLine.

---

* One of my personal all-time favorites!

Okay, let's look at a step-by-step guide for writing your mission statement as described in the Personal Leadership Application Workbook by Stephen R. Covey. Remember, a mission statement is as much discovery as it is creation. Don't rush it or set rigid timetables for yourself; rather, go slowly through the process, answer the questions below (and any others that you can think of specifically for yourself), and think deeply about your values and aspirations.

Step 1 Identify Your Influential Person

An effective way to focus on what you want to be and do is to identify a highly influential individual in your life and think about how this individual has contributed to your life. This person may be a parent, work associate, friend, family member, or neighbor. Answer the following questions, keeping in mind your personal goals, i.e. what you want to be and do within the context of your MLM company.

- Who has been one of the most influential people in my life?
- Which qualities do I most admire in that person?
- What qualities have I gained (or do I desire to gain) from that person?

Step 2 Define What You Want to *Be*, and *Do*, and *Have*

A meaningful mission contains three basic elements.

- The first is what you want to *be* -- what character strengths do you want to have, what qualities do you want to develop?

106

- The second is what you want to **do** -- what do you want to accomplish? What contributions do you want to make?
- The third is what you want to **have** -- what possessions, money, and *things* do you wish to have?

It is relatively easy to identify the things we want to have; for many of us, that list will be the longest. It's important to keep in mind, however, that legitimate power and the highest levels of human happiness and fulfillment originate from *be*ing, not having!

Ponder the following questions with deep thought and sincere reflection and write out your revelations in your journal.

- What I'd like to **be***:*

- What I'd like to **do***:*

- What I'd like to **have***:*

Step 3 Define your Life Roles

We live our lives in terms of roles—not only in the sense of role-playing but in the sense of authentic parts we have chosen to fill. You may have roles in work, in family, in community, and many other areas of your life. These roles become a natural framework that give order to what you want to do and to be. For example, you may see yourself as a wife/mother, a sales manager, a community advocate, a United Way Chairperson, a friend. You may divide your life into family, society, finances, keeping your body healthy, your mind healthy, and growing spiritually.

Whatever your roles look like, define and list up to seven personal and/or professional life roles. After you've created the list, sit quietly and project yourself forward in time. Visualize the important people in your life describing you as you would most like to be described in each role. This may take a bit of time. That's okay – make the time needed, because you are worth it! Remember, don't rush yourself. After you've seen and heard your most favorable description, write it next to each role.

By identifying your life roles, you will gain perspective and balance. By writing these descriptive statements, you will begin to visualize your highest self. You will also identify the core principles and values by which you desire to live. Never underestimate the power of your mind in the act of creating your dreams!

Step 4 Write a Draft of Your Mission Statement

Now that you have identified your life roles and defined what you want to be and do, you are prepared to begin working on your personal mission statement. Create a rough draft, drawing heavily upon the thinking you've done in the previous three steps. Carry this draft with you and make notes, additions, and deletions before you attempt another draft. Your final blueprint may take a week, or a month, or a year; keep at it until it "feels" right, don't settle–keep climbing.

Step 5 Evaluate

Don't let your statement become outdated. Periodic review and evaluation can help you keep in touch with your own development and keep your statement in harmony with your deepest self. This is very important and, speaking from personal experience, difficult. It takes discipline and desire to get in the habit of regular and frequent reviews - do it! As you journal about your MLM life, take an hour (perhaps on a quarterly basis) and ask yourself these questions:

- Is my mission based on timeless, proven principles? Which ones?
- Do I feel this mission statement represents the best possible me?
- During my best moments, do I feel good about what this mission statement represents?
- Do I feel my direction, purpose, challenge, and motivation when I review this statement?
- Am I aware of the strategies and skills that will help me accomplish what I have written?
- What do I need to start doing right now to be where I want to be tomorrow?

The final test of the value and effectiveness of a mission statement is:

Does this statement inspire me?

Step 6 Write a Permanent Draft

As suggested in Step 5, it is recommended that you keep a rough draft of your mission statement for a while to revise and evaluate. Be sure it inspires the best within you. When you develop what you feel is a permanent draft of your statement, review it frequently (quarterly perhaps). I strongly urge you to commit it to memory so that you keep your vision and your values clearly in mind. When you're tempted to worry, replay your mission statement instead.

And finally . . .

Now I'm about to let you in on what was a secret to me until I wrote this book. Mission Statements are important *and* there are several high-profile companies that do not have them! What? Yup. I don't know why, but Sears, Apple Computer, Ford Motor Company, Harley-Davidson, Inc.* and many others have not etched a statement of mission into stone, onto copy paper or anywhere else I know about!

Here's my only request of you: Please exert great effort in writing your statement. I mean give it a genuine push. The process can be an exhausting and lengthy undertaking as well as an exhilarating and enlivening adventure. Along the way, you just might produce thoughts and statements that for the first time in your life ring true . . . give you direction . . . put a smile on your face.

---

* Notice, these companies are currently experiencing financial difficulties; perhaps they *need* a mission statement.

If you honestly cannot write a mission statement and you're sure you want to do this thing called MLM, **GO FOR IT!** If Apple Computer and other companies can make it *sans* mission statement, perhaps you can to. Whatever you do, remember to enjoy the journey.[*]

---

[*] I know I've suggested this before, but I cannot help myself—I must say it again. Get together with your leaders or those who might one day be leaders and/or your upline. Carve out a half-day workshop. Hire a facilitator to guide you through the process of writing a Mission Statement. To get the most for your money, do the above exercises before the workshop. It might cost you $1,000 (divide that between five or six associates). It will definitely cost some time and it might send you off on the adventure of your life-time!

June 24 ~ I'm frustrated, fractious, and contrary today. I have been marching to the company tune for months, I've reached the Silver level, and I can't seem to get my downline motivated. What's up? Every day I think of ways to tell my MLM-story to new people, yet my downline find reasons to put it off until tomorrow. If I am ever to receive 'residual' income I have to find a way to help my success-line succeed. How?

June 26 - shortly after I wrote those depressing words in my journal, I discovered an article written by Randolph Byrd titled The $300 Solution. Funny how I've found that when you ask for help and then pay attention the answer always appears - it's a rule - it always appears.

The past year and a few months has taught me "the only way to fail is to quit." But I'm having trouble convincing the people in my Network about that. How do I get them to stay involved long enough to start seeing some success? This is one of those hard to answer questions that comes up again and again in my mind - there are lots of great ways to answer it. Making sure your people are motivated by helping them stay clear on what their own personal goals are, making sure they have the tools they need and know how to use them, making sure their efforts are supported by three-way calls and meetings until they've got their 'sea-legs' securely under them, all these are sound approaches. So what's missing?

Well, according to Randolph Byrd, the missing element is basic and essential. It's MONEY! So what are the conditions I've got to create for my people to get them involved and keep them involved?

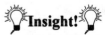
Insight!
Money is the root of all evil?!?
The actual quote is: *"It's the Love of Money that's the root of all evil."*

THE $300 SOLUTION?

What follows is Byrd's actual article* along with my observations inserted here and there. Enjoy!

There are two things which prevent most Network Marketers from achieving success: (1) they don't make $300.00 per month quickly enough, and (2) their downline distributors don't either! Surprised? You're not alone; so was I. But the truth is that $300.00 is the income-earning threshold below which there is simply no Network Marketing Sales Organization. Without a $300.00 per month check there are simply no MLMers to make your organization a team! People who make $300.00 a month in this business stick around. People who don't – don't. It's that simple.

The MLM number one enemy is – ATTRITION. No one in this profession likes to talk about attrition. Why not? Because it undermines the profession's primary positive benefit which we all recite in our prospecting routines. You know the rap: *"You sponsor 10 people, and they sponsor 10 people, and they . . . and pretty soon . . ."*

---

* This article can be found on the World Wide Web in the Upline Online Library (http://www.upline.com) and it's free. Upline magazine (804) 979-4427, also has professionally printed copies available at reasonable rates.

Now, how successful would you be as a prospector if you said instead: *"You sponsor 10 people, and then nine of them drop out, and then the one who's left sponsors 10 people and nine of them will drop out, and then . . ."* Doesn't sound like much of a positive proactive pitch, now, does it? Yet this is the truth – or at least, it has been for most Network Marketers.

Please note that when we say 'attrition', we're not just talking about the downline, that impersonal genealogy of all the distributors in your organization. We're talking about *you* – one individual Network Marketer. Statistically, attrition rates in Network Marketing average about 80 to 90 percent per year. That means eight or nine out of every ten distributors drop out of their organizations (and most of those drop out of Networking Sales altogether). This happens within a year or less of signing on. Factually, that's no different than mainstream business startups, where eight or nine out of ten new businesses fail within the first year of operation!

What really hurts is that an 80-to-90 percent attrition rate means 80-to-90 percent of all your efforts as well as all the efforts of your downline organization are lost in spinning your wheels, i.e. sponsoring numbers of folks into your organization only to have them leave before they've had the chance to be successful! As Dayle Maloney says, "The problem with most Network Marketers is that they quit before payday."

What causes this high drop-out rate? And what can we do about it? Ask open-ended questions like those above and you're bound to get long, equally open-ended answers. CEOs and master distributors alike have given us all sorts of philosophies on why distributors leave our profession. I'll mention some of those reasons in a bit, but to find the empirical 'truth', let's rephrase the question -- *At what point do Network Marketers NOT drop out of their organizations?* Specifically, how many dollars per month in compensation does an MLMer have to earn before a high percentage (let's say, 95 percent) do NOT drop out?

According to Byrd, here are the answers:

- How much do you have to make? Just about all we spoke with answered:
  "$300 to $400 per month, sustained for at least two or three months."

- And 'by when' do they have to make that amount?
  "Six to nine months is best, with one year being the longest time allotted."

- And what if they don't?
  "They leave the organization at a rate of 80 to 90 percent per year."

- And if they do achieve $300.00 per month?
  "They stay on board and usually become even more successful."

Now think about this. This "law" is true for you, the individual distributor, just as it is true for your downline, a group of individual distributors just like you. Have yourself -- and have each of your downline – receive $300.00 or more per month in bonus compensation within six to nine months, and you will all stay in the organization and produce! By the way, retail profits don't count in this scenario, because the whole point is 'residual' income. Your downline will be certain to stay the course if you teach the 'truth' about this business to them. This duplicable system is as easy as distributing copies of this Report to each person in your downline.

NEXT QUESTION?

So why don't most Network Marketers ever get to the $300.00 per month level? Perhaps poor prospecting/sponsoring, and lack of knowledge about this industry and how Network Marketing Sales really works, all of which leads to unrealistic expectations. The way you prospect and sponsor each individual into your program sets up their expectation for success . . . or for failure.

A common approach to prospecting/sponsoring is the 'pie-in-the-sky, get rich quick, let your downline do the work while you stroll the beaches of the world' routine. This method can set up your new distributor for failure almost immediately, because the truth is that 98 percent of all Network Marketers do not ever reach those heights -- and most certainly do not do so within just a year. This 'lottery' mentality creates beguiling dreams about what this business has to offer and then just as quickly dashes them. With this style of prospecting/sponsoring, even if a distributor did reach $300.00 per month, they'd probably feel like a big failure, because they were set up to make $30,000 a month, not $300.00.

We have a common misconception in this business that $300.00 is such small potatoes, it's not even worth mentioning; just so much chopped liver. Well, think about this. $300.00 per month invested at a 10% return for 10 years will grow to over $62,000; enough to get one child into his/her senior year at college!

Tom "Big Al" Schreiter (MLM success story and trainer) relates a wonderful story about a man who came into the business with the goal of making $300.00 a month. Not $10,000 or $20,000, just $300.00 a month. The man achieved that goal fairly easily and stayed at the $300.00 income level for a number of years. That didn't seem very ambitious to Tom -- especially for such an obviously gifted and capable guy -- so, he asked the fellow about it. The man told Tom that he took his initial $300 and accelerated the mortgage payment on his home, paying if off in record time. He then used his free-and-clear equity to buy a second property, rented it out, and applied the 'extra' $300.00 in the same manner he had with his own house. In less than five years, he owned five income properties, financially set for the rest of his life. All by virtue of the $300.00 a month he earned through Network Marketing Sales.

What other common miscommunications do MLM prospectors often make?

> *"You won't have to work for a living."*
> *"You can become a millionaire like my upline."*
> (Flash a copy of upline's mega-check here.)
> *"Network Marketing the answer to all your financial woes."*
> *"MLM can fulfill all your dreams."*

While none of these statements are outright lies, and are often true for a few leadership distributors, they do set up false expectations for the novice Networker. Instead, use statements like, "Network Marketing Sales can offer you greater time-freedom as you can work this business anywhere, anytime you choose." Or, "You can achieve a part-time or full-time income that can supplement or replace your current source of income, making enough in a few hours a week to pay for your car loan, a college education, etc." When linked to your prospect's 'why,' these statements set up value in the opportunity without creating unrealistic expectations for what this business has to offer.

Enter *The $300 Solution*

Now, what would happen if you told your downline (or your upline had told you!) that the first step to MLM success is to get to the $300.00 a month level within six to nine months – or maybe even a year? What happens to their expectations now? What would happen if you told them the truth about this business: When a distributor reaches a monthly compensation bonus of $300.00 per month, he/she will not drop out! This is a point of no return! There is no turning back! When that $300.00 level is reached, you and/or your organization MUST recognize and acknowledge their level of achievement. After all, in this recognition business, $300.00 a month is a 'rite of passage.' Call it a coming of age and celebrate it like a bar or bas mitzvah. Like puberty was for each of us, it becomes a point of no return! It is a bridge into MLM adulthood where one may not ever return to being a child!

Celebrating this MLM Coming of Age, you set up a great expectation for your entire group. Imagine for a moment that you told your downline that the amount necessary to achieve the no-going-back level was $2,000.00 instead of the real $300.00? The $300.00 milestone would go by unnoticed, as their expectation is $2000.00 for the first level of real achievement and success. Now imagine sharing *The $300 Solution* with them and making a public celebration out of every distributor's achieving this level. They will not drop out because they've learned to expect that distributors earning $300.00 monthly **do not quit!**[*] Once the truth about this business is clear, everyone will operate within that truth! It will become a Law of Network Marketing Sales Nature.

So, how do we get to that magical $300-per-month benchmark? You and your downline are halfway there already, because you are now armed with the knowledge of *The $300 Solution.* Since most new Network Marketers haven't a clue as to how this profession works, they usually don't know what's expected of them. They have no realistic goal. Perhaps their goal is not specific. It probably has no basis in fact even if they do have one. With this new paradigm, they can have a realistic goal that's achievable, backed up by research about this new business they have joined. They now can have realistic expectations for themselves, and for their future downline, too!

As for the specifics of how to get them to the $300.00 level in your organization, that depends somewhat on your products and your compensation plan. So, do a little research on your own program and establish several scenarios for your distributor group. Teach them how to get to $300 a month as soon as possible! Help your downline members get to this level by prospecting and sponsoring distributors with them. In all MLM companies, partnership is the key. Come to think of it, *partnering* is a way of living successfully. Three-way calling and three-way sponsoring interviews are powerful partnering tools you can use

---

[*] Note also the difference in their attitude when they achieve only $150 per month. Within the old paradigm of 'getting rich,' $150 would have left them feeling like, and therefore, being a failure. Now, when they reach $150, they'll say, "I'm halfway home" What a difference!

to have almost anybody at $300.00 in a very quick time.* What's more, if they use three-ways with all their people the way you did with them, imagine the dependability and duplicability of that!

If you want more of your people to stick with it -- and with you, too -- inject *The $300 Solution* into your teaching and training routine. Don't be afraid that you will scare off those 'heavy hitters' with an eye to more sky-high incomes. Those folks will clearly and quickly see the virtue of a system that has hundreds and hundreds of part-time networkers all earning enough to keep them in the business.

Just for fun -- and for the present and future possibilities of profit -- take out your calculator and crunch some numbers to see what would happen if you were to diminish your own organization's attrition rate by, say, 10 or 20 percent. I think that you'll find what you've got there, in terms of your own check, is a good deal more than $300.

---

* Consistency is vital . . . one week of 3-ways will not a success create!

July 4 -I've read The $300 Solution
article twice in the past few days - there's a
lot to think about. During my short stint as
a Networker, I've mostly seen and heard
about the enormous sums of money one can
make in this business. At the week-end
training I attended last year I developed a
belief that I would be making $10,000 per
month before the end of my first summer.
Now, after over a year in the trenches and
knowledge of The $300 solution, I'm
thinking my goal was unrealistic. Not the
amount, I'm certain I can earn that kind
of income, but perhaps my time-line was too
short. And, perhaps I would have felt better
about my progress if I'd been primed to
expect incremental successes along the way.
I would have been "re-charged" if my upline
had acknowledged me at $300 per month,
then $800 per month and so forth. If every
one in my downline was earning $300.00 a
month, I'd be a happy climber (I'm not a
camper!). Let me be more realistic; if only
2-out-5 in my organization consistently

earned $300.00 per month I'd be delighted. So, the question is "should I lower my sights and help my Success Line achieve a first level goal of only $300.00 per month?"

July 8 - I am troubled about how to reconcile Mr. Hock's noble expectation* with Byrd's $300 Solution? It's not unreasonable for me to expect to earn $10,000 or more per month - right now that is all that I might dream. The $300 Solution is step one in a series of steps toward that dream. Instead of attempting a giant leap-frog jump from the bottom step to the middle (perhaps breaking my leg in the process), employing the $300 solution will build me a solid base of consistent money earners and, with style and dignity, I will climb each step one at a time?

Insight!

*... it is no failure to fall short of realizing all that we might dream. The failure is to fall short of dreaming all that we might realize.

✍ Dee Hock

HOBBY OR REAL BUSINESS?

As with any legitimate business venture, reliable full-time incomes may involve several months of hard work, perhaps even at an initial loss. But an up-front investment of only a few hundred dollars does provide a very real opportunity to earn a few hundred dollars back each month in residual income, perhaps for life. Many conservative network marketers build their businesses only to the point of earning $200 - $300 per month. That same, small additional income will provide a comfortable, secure retirement for most if properly invested–an agenda championed by many wise upline network marketers today. It is my belief, after eighteen months of observation, that the likelihood of accomplishing enormous wealth in MLM is similar to winning the lottery; but it is commonplace today to find comfortable livings or supplemental incomes being earned by those who take the business seriously. And the great part of the new paradigm is I don't have employees, office overhead, a long commute, inventory, or accounting to take care of (my MLM does that for me).

Now that you know about *The $300 Solution*, consider how you might adjust your prospecting. Or, how you might pull together your existing group and hold a $300 Solution training. This could infuse great excitement into the future of your MLM organization.

Businesses, as well as races, tribes and nations, die out NOT *when they are defeated or suppressed, but when they become despairing and lose excitement and hope about the future.*

✍ Dee Hock

July 15 - Talked with Jack again today. He's sad and disappointed and frustrated and yet he keeps on keeping on! He told me he was sorry he'd given up his primary source of cash-flow so soon to do MLM. His enthusiasm, the sales training (external motivation), and his desire to leave a boring job, got the better of him and he thought (believed!) nothing could stop him from climbing to the top - and quick! His money ran out before he got to first base-camp and he had to 'eat-crow' (his words). He was forced to go back into the corporate world at a significantly lower salary. Both his self-esteem and wallet were hurt. Today, he still works his MLM (part time) in the hopes of getting out of the American Rat Race. I wonder how many people 'jump' into MLM too soon, leaving behind the necessity of a paycheck, while they climb the networking ladder? I wonder if this is a reason for the high attrition rate?

Until one is committed there is hesitance, the chance to draw back, always ineffectiveness.

Concerning all acts of initiative (and creation) there is one elementary truth, the ignorance of which kills countless ideas and splendid plans;

That the moment one definitely commits oneself, then providence moves too.

All sorts of things occur to help one that would otherwise never have occurred.

A whole stream of events issues from the decision, raising in one's favor all manner of unforeseen incidents and meetings and material assistance, which no man could have dreamt would have come his way.

≥W.N. Murray, 1951

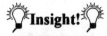

Insight!

**Commitment, desire, persistence, and
determination will pay off. But until it does,
hold on to your day job, your primary source
of cash flow! Start off by dedicating a couple
of hours per week in your MLM and slowly,
as you experience success, add more time to
networking. Eventually, you may be able to
devote one hundred percent of your time to
your MLM entrepreneurial dream.**

DON'T QUIT YOUR DAY JOB!

As a result of MLM I have learned a deep respect for one of Goethe's couplets:

> *"Whatever you can do, or dream you can — begin it -- boldness has genius, power and magic in it."*

The above concept and the quote on page 129 by Murray (a mountain climber no less!) are used to influence you to seriously consider jumping into MLM with 100% of your effort. The words are noble, weighty, and persuasive. I believe them! It is true that when one makes a commitment and becomes mindful of his/her environment a *"...whole stream of events issues from the decision raising in one's favor..."*

Lots of books are being written these days on the topic of personal power and responsibility. In *Conversations with God - Book 1* the author, Neale Walsch, gives us much to ponder regarding the connection between commitment and accomplishment.

> *So go ahead. Ask Me anything. Anything. I will contrive to bring you the answer. The whole universe will I use to do this. So be on the lookout; this book is far from My only tool. You may ask a question, then put this book down. But watch. Listen. The words to the next song you hear. The information in the next article you read. The story line of the next movie you watch. The chance utterance of the next person you meet. Or the whisper of the next river, the next ocean, the next breeze that caresses your ear—all these devices are Mine; all these avenues are open to Me. I will speak to you if you will listen. I will come to you if you will invite Me. I will show you than that I have always been there. All ways.*

Realizing one's dreams is, *partly*, a matter of making the commitment and then listening, watching, and feeling your environment for clues that show you 'how-to' accomplish those dreams. Remember our discussion about intuition and that sixth sense?

I say partly because I believe that timing is also a very important element! Don't quit your day job or abandon your primary source of income until the time-is-right. When is that you ask? There are many ways to answer that question: perhaps it's when you have sustained a certain level of MLM income for several months, or you're willing to begin investing your savings while your MLM-business grows, or . . . you fill in the blank. I have no doubt you will know when the time is right. If you ask, and then listen, The Department of Angels will respond.

At a recent Monday morning meeting this 'timing' issue was made clear to me by one of my company's top-earners. He made a statement about "ABC" (Always Be Closing). The message came across to me that, in order to be successful you must always be recruiting -- "it's vital to keep bringing in new distributors." Financially successful MLMers *do* MLM full time! Again, look around and observe what the 'big-hitters' do everyday. They recruit!

With a 97% (or higher) attrition rate, they have to recruit to keep earning. Don't get me wrong, MLM is an economically sound and exciting way to spend your time here on Planet Earth. Yet, be careful as to when you commit yourself 'full time'. This book is about helping you see the smorgasbord of available options in this game so that you increase your likelihood of success however you define it. Timing is one of those options.

*Heavy silence fills
the room and points to me;
I spoke the truth too soon.*

--✍ William Warriner

EPILOGUE

When I look into the future, it's so bright it burns by eyes.
✍ Oprah Winfrey

For sometime now I have been putting off the completion of this book. Why? My first excuse is that I don't know what I'll do when this book is finished. Is it back to MLM prospecting, training downline, retailing my product? Or has my vision of the future changed because of this book? I don't know . . .

The second evasion is born out of my fear of not knowing how to smoothly put the finishing touches on *Confessions*.

My Myers-Briggs type (INFP) prefers not to close up this final chapter; if I stay open just a little longer more information will come to me – information important to you perhaps as well!

Most epilogues seem to sum-up the previous pages with some pithy remarks, or they offer advice about how to use the information presented. My closing remarks are questions aimed at you! I hope you got a flash of insight about who you are and what you want to do with your life. If it's MLM, great! If it's not, great!

I do not have a vested interest in your being an MLMer. I *do* have a vested interest in your being authentic and genuine and happy. That might sound curious since there's a good chance I don't know you. I believe that every individual has a responsibility to expect others to achieve their highest and best possibilities. It's up to each person to do their own "work" and it's up to me to do mine! To cheer you on and encourage you is part of my work.

I accept the fact that we are all connected and consequently, what you feel and do affects me. So, of course, I want you to feel really good.

> *All things are connected.*
> *Whatever befalls the Earth,*
> *Befalls the children of the Earth.*
> ✍ Chief Seattle

Eighteen months ago I started writing in my journal about my excitement, hopes for the future and frustrations about this business. Then, without my permission, it "morphed" into this publication. When I took off the blinders and became open to all that life and the universe had to offer, strange and unexplainable events happened. When you do take off the blinders, you receive that which you are ready for; however, you can receive it only if you recognize it. With the blinders on (a metaphor for the old paradigm of control and command), life may offer you success, but you may not see it–and your struggle will continue. If you relax just a bit, perhaps your organization will resort to the theory of *morphology* and grow without your permission into something beautiful.

I have come to love this creative and creating industry despite it's blemishes or maybe even because of them. After all, these weaknesses are the challenges that give each and everyone of us our opportunities. Robin Norwood once said "every problem is an assignment from your soul." Will you rise to the challenge, whatever it is? *Climb* the mountain, wherever it is? All events, all experiences, create opportunity. It is what we think of them, do about them, how we respond to them, that gives them meaning.

A final challenge. . .

As I experience the journey of building my MLM organization and reflect on what I've written in these pages, a new and radical thought emerges and jumps onto this page. It has become apparent to me that creating a MLM downline might have to be based on biological concepts and methods. This organization would have to 'self' evolve, in effect to invent and organize itself without intervention from the upline. Radical? Yes!

How about it? Could you let it evolve, unfold, emerge without your command and control? In *A Simpler Way* by Margaret Wheatley and Myron Kellner-Rogers, the authors invite the reader to believe that the mechanistic image of the world no longer helps us. It is their belief, and mine, that there is *a simpler way* to organize human endeavor. It requires a new way of being, thinking and believing in the world. It demands being in the world **without fear**. Being in the world with play and creativity. Seeking after what's possible. Being willing to learn and to be surprised.

Wheatley and Kellner-Rogers are corporate management consultants. They seem to specialize in thinking and teaching about how the future might be different if we do not base the future on the past. Faith Popcorn, in the *Popcorn Report* also seems to look into the future without looking backward. In both books the authors ask and postulate many unusual thoughts – unusual because they think outside the box. I've adopted some of the ideas from *a simpler way* to the future of MLM, what do you think?

- This *simpler way* to organize MLM requires a belief that the world is inherently orderly. The world seeks organization. It does not need us humans to organize it.

- This *simpler way* summons forth what is best about us. It asks us to understand human nature differently, more optimistically. It identifies us as creative. It acknowledges that we seek meaning. It asks us to be less serious, yet more purposeful, about our work and our lives. It does not separate play from the nature of being.

- This world of a *simpler way* is a world we already know. We may not have seen it clearly, but we have been living in it all our lives. It is a world that is more welcoming, more hospitable to our humanness. Who we are and what is best about us can more easily flourish in a simpler way.

The world is not a machine. It is alive, filled with life and the history of life. Whenever we discover ancient rocks, notes biologist James Lovelock, we also discover ancient life preserved in them. Life cannot be eradicated from the world, even though our machine metaphors have tried.

As we change our images of the world, as we leave behind the machine, we welcome ourselves back, we re-member. We recover a world that is supportive of human endeavor.

This is life's invitation to freedom, creativity, and meaning. And MLM is advertised as a place to experience freedom, creativity, and meaning. Seems to me *our* industry is evolving away from the machine metaphor and toward a simpler way, would you not agree?

If we can be in the world in the fullness of our humanity, what are we capable of? If we are free to play, to experiment and discover, if we are free to fail (what an idea, eh?), what might we create? What could we accomplish if we stopped trying to structure the world into existence? What could we accomplish if we worked with life's natural tendency to organize? Who could we be if we found a simpler way?

So, I ask you again – will you build your MLM organization with command and control or will you build it in this simpler way? It may be more a challenge to "let go and trust" and yet the journey may indeed be richer!

Several years ago I climbed Mt. Adams in Washington State. It was my first 'real' mountain and I remember my feelings vividly. I got up at 1:30 in the morning! Having camped at the 10,000 foot level that night, before me lay only a couple thousand feet of hard work. I was both excited and fresh from a good night's sleep. The sounds were sharper than in the city, the colors were clearer and cleaner, the stars were so bright that I was able to see the footpath without using my flashlight. It was cold! Later, around 10:00 AM (after eight and a half hours of putting one heavy boot in front of the other equally heavy boot), I saw the summit, only 800 more feet–straight up! I remember how that sight thrilled me. I let out a yelp that sounded a little like an eagle's cry. Seeing the pinnacle seemed to give me renewed energy and the power to push ahead, to reach down deep inside to achieve my goal. Ninety minutes later I stood on that summit — I nearly cried when I learned it was the *false summit* of Mt. Adams! There was yet more climbing to do if I was to make it to the 'real' top of the mountain.[*]

Working in MLM, for me, is like climbing Mt. Adams. You set your goal and begin the ascent, all the while believing that when you arrive it will be over. In reality, each time you clear a peak, on the horizon is a view so beautiful you must continue the climb. The trick is to know that success lies in every step, that every time you make contact with the earth you experience success. As humans, we are pulled forward to the next peak to see what we have not yet seen. We may *learn* to hesitate, to camp, perhaps even to quit; yet I believe our nature is to climb.

One of my favorite quotes from T. S. Eliot goes like this:

> *We must not cease from exploration. And the end of all our exploring will be to arrive where we began and know the place for the first time.*

Keep exploring, keep climbing, and I bet I'll see you at the top!

---

[*] For those of you who are curious, I did make it to the top! I even planted the flag.

ADDENDUM

Now it's your turn. I would really like to hear from you. In the words of a very successful MLMer, "tell me what you liked best."

You pick your method of communication: fax, phone, email or regular mail! I'll look forward to your insights and I promise to respond.

Thank you,

Patrick

Post script: My next MLM book is about couples and partners working together. It's about the challenges, struggles, successes, etc. The material will be in the form of actual interviews and stories submitted to me. If you're interested in telling your "couple-power*" story, send it to me as soon as possible.

Patrick Snetsinger
1075 Bellevue Way NE, Suite 124
Bellevue, WA 98004
MLMTrainer@aol.com
Phone 800-936-7114 ~ (425) 646-1040 ~ Fax (425) 454-1040

---

* Couple Power is a term used by Cardell and Liz Smith in The Power Seminars, (714) 631-9151.

BIBLIOGRAPHY

I used several outside sources in writing *Confessions,* most of which I cited within the referenced paragraph. These are all listed below.

I also know in my heart-of-hearts that I've used or paraphrased other authors' words and concepts, perhaps without proper acknowledgment. I think this can happen when the ideas of many writers begin to blend in one's mind. (Who's idea was that? I sometimes ask after reading something I just wrote.)

In an effort to give credit where credit is due, I also include in this bibliography all the books I believe a serious MLMer might want in her/his library – books I'm sure that in one way or another have influenced this book.

- Abrahams, Jeffrey. *The Mission Statement Book.* Ten Speed Press, 1995.
- Bellman, Geoffrey. *The Consultant's Calling.* Jossey-Bass, 1990.
- Bennett, Hal Zina. *Invitation to Success.* Tenacity Press, 1997.
- Bristol, Claude. *The Magic of Believing.* Simon & Schuster, 1985.
- Clason, George. *The Richest Man in Babylon.* A Signet Book, 1955.
- Covey, Stephen. *The 7 Habits of Highly Effective People.* Fireside/Simon & Schuster, Inc., 1989.
- Fogg, John Milton. *The Greatest Networker in the World.* MLM Publishing, Inc., 1992
- Gibran Kahlil. *The Prophet.* Alfred A. Knopf Publishers, New York, 1923.
- Hill, Napoleon. *Think & Grow Rich.* A Plum Book, 1990.
- Hirsch, Peter. *Living With Passion.* MLM Publishing, Inc., 1994.

- Jones, Laurie Beth. *The Path.* New York: Hyperion, 1996.
- Kalench, John. *17 Secrets of the Master Prospectors.* MIM Publications, 1994.
- Kalench, John. *Being the Best You Can Be in MLM.* MIM Publications, 1990.
- Myss, Caroline. *Anatomy of the Spirit.* New York: Harmony Books, 1996.
- Nadler, Beverly. *Congratulations . . . You Lost Your Job!.* MLM Publishing, Inc., 1992.
- Naparstek, Belleruth. *Your Sixth Sense.* HarperSanFrancisco, 1997.
- Needleman, Jacob. *Money and the Meaning of Life.* Doubleday Currency, 1991.
- Poe, Richard. *The Wave 3 Way to Building Your Downline.* Prima Publishing, 1997.
- Poe, Richard. *Wave 3 - The New Era In Network Marketing.* Prima Publishing, 1994.
- Popcorn, Faith. *The Popcorn Report.* HarperBusiness, 1991.
- Stoltz, Paul. *Adversity Quotient - Turning Obstacles into Opportunities.* Wiley & Sons, 1997
- Walsch, Neale Donald. *Conversations with God - an uncommon dialogue - book 1.* New York: G.P. Putnam's Sons, 1995.
- Walsch, Neale Donald. *Conversations with God - an uncommon dialogue - book 2.* Hampton Roads, 1997.
- Warriner, William. *101 Corporate Haiku.* Addison-Wesley, 1994.
- Wheatley, Margaret & Kellner-Rogers, Myron. *a simpler way.* Barrett-Koehler Publishers, 1996.
- Whyte, David. *The Heart Aroused.* Currency Doubleday, 1994.